Making Sense

SKILLS FOR ACTIVE READERS

Green

RL: 4-7

Senior Editor	Terry Ofner
Project Editors	Pegi Bevins
	Cecelia Munzenmaier
	Shawn Simmons
Permissions/Research	Cynthia M. Martin
Art Director	Randy Messer
Designer	Jan M. Michalson
Reviewers	Penny Beers, Ed.D.
	English and Reading Program Planner
	School District of Palm Beach County
	West Palm Beach, Florida
	Charles J. Shields
	English Department Chairman
	Homewood-Flossmore High School
	Flossmore, Illinois
	Robin Willis
	Reading Specialist
	Riverside Indian School
	Anakarko, Oklahoma

© 1998 Perfection Learning Corporation
1000 North Second Avenue, P.O. Box 500, Logan, Iowa 51546-1099

ISBN 0-7891-2334-7
Printed in the U.S.A.

Table of Contents

Fiction

Short Stories allow you to see the world through another person's eyes.

Myths and Folktales provide answers to basic human questions and teach important lessons.

Poetry

Poets play with words and ideas to create interesting pictures. Read these poems and join in the fun!

Table of Contents

Table of Contents

Information cont.

Science and Technology
Test the scientific thinking of these authors.

Social Studies
What was it like to survive a battle or experience the coming of the first American settlers?

BECOMING AN ACTIVE READER

Active readers don't just read—they interact with what they read. Active readers focus their attention on what they are reading and use strategies like the ones below.

Active Reading Strategies

- **Ask questions**—Active readers question anything they wonder about or don't understand. For example, if an active reader reads that the main character is going to "go a-courtin'," that reader might ask "I wonder what you do when you go a-courtin'?" An active reader would then be on the lookout for clues that would answer that question.

- **Make predictions**—Active readers predict what might happen based on the information in the story. An active reader who is reading a survival story, for example, might predict that the characters will miss a chance at being rescued.

- **Clarify**—Active readers look for answers to their questions and predictions. Once their questions and predictions are clarified, active readers gain a better understanding of the text.

- **Make connections**—Active readers relate what they are reading to their own knowledge and experience. For example, an active reader who is reading about a dog might compare that animal to a favorite pet.

- **Evaluate**—Active readers draw conclusions about what they have read. By evaluating a selection, active readers are able to form their own opinions about characters, actions, and the selection as a whole.

- **Determine the meanings of new words**—Active readers try to figure out what new words mean. They may look in a dictionary, examine the different parts of the word, or read the surrounding text for clues.

- **React personally**—Active readers comment on different aspects of the text according to their own beliefs and attitudes. An active reader might decide that a certain character is selfish or generous, based on the reader's personal feelings.

A good way to understand a selection is to combine the **Active Reading Strategies** with the **Think-Along** method. Readers who "think along" jot down their thoughts as they read. An example of the Think-Along method is provided on the next page. Look in the right-hand column to see what one student was thinking as she read "Wish for Power." What questions or comments would you add to the Think-Along?

WISH FOR POWER

Adapted from a Chinese Folktale

Think-Along

There was once a stonecutter who was known for his skill at carving statues. He took pride in his work and earned just enough money to pay for the things he needed—a simple home and food for his table. He enjoyed the respect of his customers and the good will of his neighbors. In short, he lived an honorable and pleasant life. Yet the stonecutter considered himself to be a very poor man.

One evening as he was working on a statue of the God of Wealth, he stepped back to survey his work. "This is my best creation yet," he said. "But tomorrow when I deliver it to the temple, I will be paid my usual trivial wage instead of the riches I deserve. Ah, the life of a poor man is filled with hard work and despair. How I wish I were a rich man instead!"

*Folktales are often about common people who make wishes. (**Making connections**)*

The next morning an amazing sight greeted the stonecutter when he awoke. The statue was bedecked with fine jewelry made of gold and precious gems. The God of Wealth had heard his prayer!

*bedecked with jewels—must mean "covered" (**Determining the meaning of a new word**)*

It did not take the stonecutter long to accept his new fortune. "Now that I am a rich man, I must live in a grand house," he declared. So he sold the jewels and bought the finest mansion in the village, complete with a staff of servants. Then he bought the most splendid clothing he could find.

Many of his neighbors began to resent the former stonecutter. They remembered when he lived a peasant's life. But he was too busy enjoying his life as a rich man to care.

*I can't blame them. He's being rather inconsiderate. (**Reacting personally**)*

One day as he was strolling through the village, he noticed a flurry of activity.

"The mandarin[1] is coming!" shouted a peasant. "Bow down!" Everyone except the rich man bowed to the mandarin as he passed.

*The footnote says a mandarin is a public official. (**Determining the meaning of a new word**)*

The mandarin noticed the rich man's impudence. "You there," he called. "Do you not know that I am a mandarin?"

"Yes, but why should I bow to you?" asked the rich man. "After all, I am a man of enormous wealth!"

*He seems to be taking his wealth a little too far here. This usually means trouble in folktales. (**Making predictions**)*

[1]A public official in China.

His pride angered the mandarin. "Guards, seize that man!" he ordered. "Give him a beating for his rudeness."

The guards grabbed the rich man and beat him soundly. Later the rich man thought about what had happened. "My money was useless against the mandarin's power," he realized. "Oh, how I wish I were a mandarin instead of just a rich man!"

The next morning, the rich man's servants arrived early to help him dress. Strangely, they carried the costume of an official of the first rank.

"What is this?" asked the puzzled rich man.

"It is your clothing, sir. You have several official events today. We thought you would want to look your finest."

The rich man wondered, "Could the gods have granted my wish? Am I indeed a mandarin?" The servants helped him into the fine cap, the violet coat, and the belt of smooth leather decorated with rubies.

"How impressive I look," he thought. "As a mandarin, I have much more power than a rich man."

The new mandarin spent the next several days strutting around the district. He made up new rules and handed out undeserved rewards and punishments. The townsfolk learned to fear and hate him. This bothered him a bit but didn't prevent him from enjoying his new, powerful position.

One morning the emperor's procession entered the village. Instantly people lowered their eyes, knowing that it was forbidden to look upon an emperor. But the mandarin sneaked a sly peek at the dazzling sight.

First came a figure carrying a yellow satin umbrella with a dragon embroidered on top. Next came the elegant sedan of the emperor, escorted by 20 men on horseback dressed in yellow satin. The procession ended with a hundred men on foot.

"This man is the highest ruler in the land," the mandarin thought. "His power is without limit. Oh, how I wish I were the emperor!" Envious and weary, he retired for the night.

The next morning, the mandarin awoke in the emperor's bedroom! Servants helped him step into imperial robes embroidered with emblems of the heavens. On his head they placed a jeweled headpiece. It was true. He was now the emperor.

I wonder how often he's going to make these wishes. (**Asking questions**)

He's letting his power go to his head. This has got to mean trouble. (**Making a prediction**)

Is he going to get in trouble like he did with the mandarin? Or is this leading to another wish? (**Asking questions**)

Aha! Another wish! (**Clarifying a question**)

He might be the emperor now, but I predict he won't be happy. (**Making a prediction**)

The new emperor enjoyed having people bow to him. Never did he tire of hearing people praise his wisdom, even when his actions were foolish or unjust. He knew they did so only out of fear or in hopes of gaining favor. But he didn't care. He rejoiced in his absolute power.

Then one hot summer day the emperor learned that even his great power had limits. The intense heat of the sun was making him sweat profusely. He was so hot that he felt as if his life would boil out of him! He ordered his men to create a breeze by waving huge fans, but it gave him no relief.

As emperor, I am helpless against the sun's power he realized. *Oh, how I wish I were the sun instead!*

> Just what I thought. He's not happy. **(Clarifying a prediction)**
>
> Why do the gods keep helping him? **(Asking a question)**

Again the gods were listening. The emperor's body shriveled up, and his spirit was transported to the sun. Now he was the Lord of the Heavens.

The new Lord of the Heavens relished his fierce power. He sent his blistering rays to scorch the land, dry up streams, and wither crops. All those who toiled beneath the sun cursed him for the heat. But he was enjoying his power too much to care about such puny, unimportant creatures.

> Power always seems to bring out meanness. **(Making a connection)**

One day as he was radiating his great heat, a heavy, dark cloud moved between him and the earth. Annoyed, the sun bellowed, "Move on! You are in my way." But the cloud stayed where it was. The sun tried to pierce the cloud with his fiery rays, but it wouldn't budge.

"My power is stupendous," the sun said. "But what's the good of having such power if a cloud can keep me from using it? Oh, how I wish I were a cloud. Then would I be content."

> He says he'll be content, but I doubt it. **(Making a prediction)**

In an instant, the gods transformed him into a huge rain cloud. Gleefully he let loose a downpour on the earth below. Rivers overflowed their banks, carrying away houses and drowning people and animals. The people prayed that the cloud would leave. But the cloud paid no attention and continued to rain on the earth.

Some days later the cloud was still enjoying his newfound power when a gust of wind began pushing him.

"Stop shoving!" the cloud snarled at the wind. But the wind kept pushing him until he was over the ocean. There he could do little harm to the land and people.

"This wind is more powerful than I," the cloud admitted. "Oh, how I wish I were the wind instead of a cloud!"

> As I predicted—this guy is never satisfied! **(Clarifying a prediction)**

Again the gods granted his wish. The wind howled with fury as he lashed the earth, blowing away huts and uprooting trees.

Suddenly the wind hit something that would not budge. It was the side of a mountain. He tried again and again, pushing with all his might, but the mountain didn't move.

Now he wants to be a mountain. What can he possibly wish for next? (Asking a question)

"Nothing is more powerful than this mountain," the wind said. "Oh, how foolish I was to want to be the wind. I wish I were a mountain instead!"

The gods nodded, and there he stood, the tallest, most massive object on Earth. He could touch the sky and see as far as the oceans. And he reflected smugly that no power on Earth could move him.

smugly—dictionary definition: in a conceited manner (Determining the meaning of a new word)

But what was that tapping sound? Tap, tap. Where was it coming from? Tap, tap, tap. He looked down and saw a stonecutter, pounding chunks of rock out of the mountain's side. Nearby were several gaping holes where other pieces had been cut out.

"Alas," the mountain said to himself, "I am immense and immovable, and yet I am being chipped away by a lowly stonecutter. Now I see that there is no power that cannot be overcome. May the gods forgive me for my foolishness! I beg to be a simple stonecutter again."

He's back to where he started. It's probably just as well. (Reacting personally)

For the last time, the gods granted his wish. He found himself back in his workshop, putting the finishing touches on his statue of the God of Wealth. He stood back and surveyed his work with satisfaction. "My skill turned a rough piece of stone into a fine statue," he said to himself. "Why should I wish for any more power than that?"

And so, for the rest of his long life, the stonecutter was content.

Great lesson: No matter who you are, there's always going to be someone "above" you. So you might as well be content with what you have. (Evaluating)

Reading Fiction

Reading a story is like putting on a pair of glasses. Authors create lenses through which we can see their world. These lenses are most obvious when two authors write about the same subject. For example, if two authors write about trains, each might create a different picture. One might present trains as destructive machines. The other might show them as a means of bringing people together.

When reading a story, the glasses created by an author often allow you to see

- the world through a character's eyes
- what someone else's life is like
- your past experiences in a new way
- familiar things as though they were brand new

QUESTIONS FOR READING FICTION

As you read the next three stories, keep the following questions in mind.

1. What does the author allow you to see and understand about the main character's life and personality?

2. How does the author treat important ideas such as individual freedom, self-control, and teamwork?

3. What parts of your own life does the author make you think about?

4. What new ideas do you have after reading the story?

5. How would you describe the view of life presented in the story—depressing? hopeful? humorous? something else?

THE DINNER PARTY

by Mona Gardner

As you read: Try to make predictions, ask questions, and look for connections in the story. Write your thoughts in the Think-Along column on the right.

Story

The country is India. A colonial official and his wife are giving a large dinner party. They are seated with their guests—army officers and government attachés and their wives, and a visiting American naturalist—in their spacious dining room, which has a bare marble floor, open rafters and wide glass doors opening onto a veranda.

A spirited discussion springs up between a young girl who insists that women have outgrown the jumping-on-a-chair-at-the-sight-of-a-mouse era and a colonel who says that they haven't.

"A woman's unfailing reaction in any crisis," the colonel says, "is to scream. And while a man may feel like it, he has that ounce more of nerve control than a woman has. And that last ounce is what counts."

Think-Along

The American does not join in the argument but watches the other guests. As he looks, he sees a strange expression come over the face of the hostess. She is staring straight ahead, her muscles contracting slightly. With a slight gesture she summons the native boy standing behind her chair and whispers to him. The boy's eyes widen: he quickly leaves the room.

Of the guests, none except the American notices this or sees the boy place a bowl of milk on the veranda just outside the open doors.

The American comes to with a start. In India, milk in a bowl means only one thing—bait for a snake. He realizes there must be a cobra in the room. He looks up at the rafters—the likeliest place—but they are bare. Three corners of the room are empty, and in the fourth the servants are waiting to serve the next course. There is only one place left—under the table.

His first impulse is to jump back and warn the others, but he knows the commotion would frighten the cobra into striking. He speaks quickly, the tone of his voice so arresting that it sobers everyone.

"I want to know just what control everyone at this table has. I will count to three hundred—that's five minutes—and not one of you is to move a muscle. Those who move will forfeit 50 rupees. Ready!"

The 20 people sit like stone images while he counts. He is saying "...two hundred and eighty..." when, out of the corner of his eye, he sees the cobra emerge and make for the bowl of milk. Screams ring out as he jumps to slam the veranda doors safely shut.

"You were right, Colonel!" the host exclaims. "A man has just shown us an example of perfect control."

"Just a minute," the American says, turning to his hostess. "Mrs. Wynnes, how did you know that cobra was in the room?"

A faint smile lights up the woman's face as she replies: "Because it was crawling across my foot."

THE DINNER PARTY

Words That Show "Nerve Control"

Directions: "The Dinner Party" is filled with words that relate to control and careful movement. Read the following passages. Try to figure out the meaning of the **bold-faced** words from the way they are used in the story. Then fill in the circle next to the correct definitions.

1. "The American does not join in the argument but watches the other guests. As he looks, he sees a strange expression come over the face of the hostess. She is staring straight ahead, her muscles **contracting** slightly."

   Ⓐ tightening

   Ⓑ violently twitching

   Ⓒ relaxing

   Ⓓ trembling

2. "With a slight **gesture** she summons the native boy standing behind her chair and whispers to him. The boy's eyes widen: he quickly leaves the room."

   Ⓐ whimper

   Ⓑ jump

   Ⓒ movement

   Ⓓ laugh

3. "The American comes to with a **start.**"

   Ⓐ shout

   Ⓑ blink

   Ⓒ jerk

   Ⓓ scare

4. "His first impulse is to jump back and warn the others, but he knows the **commotion** would frighten the cobra into striking."

   Ⓐ fear

   Ⓑ disturbance

   Ⓒ group

   Ⓓ reaction

5. "He speaks quickly, the tone of his voice so **arresting** that it sobers everyone."

   Ⓐ funny

   Ⓑ attention-getting

   Ⓒ serious

   Ⓓ recognizable

Who's in Control Here?

This story begins with two opinions about whether men or women have more control in a crisis. A young girl insists that women have outgrown the jumping-on-a-chair-at-the-sight-of-a-mouse era while the colonel insists that men have more control than women. How does the author view this question?

Directions: First describe how each character in the chart below shows control. Write your response on the right-hand side. Then answer the questions that follow.

Character	Character's Control
1. hostess	The hostess shows control by
2. American	The American shows control by
3. native boy	The native boy shows control by

4. What statement do you think best sums up the author's attitude?

Ⓐ Men have more control in a crisis situation.

Ⓑ Women are actually more in control than men.

Ⓒ Self-control depends on the individual.

Ⓓ Some women can show a surprising amount of self-control.

Your Turn

Who do you think shows the most control in this story? Explain your opinion.

JUST ONCE

by Thomas J. Dygard

As you read: Think about what it means to be a linebacker.

Everybody liked the Moose. To his father and mother he was Bryan—as in Bryan Jefferson Crawford—but to everyone at Bedford City High he was the Moose. He was large and strong, as you might imagine from his nickname, and he was pretty fast on his feet—sort of nimble, you might say—considering his size. He didn't have a pretty face but he had a quick and easy smile—"sweet," some of the teachers called it; "nice," others said.

But on the football field, the Moose was neither sweet nor nice. He was just strong and fast and a little bit devastating as the left tackle of the Bedford City Bears. When the Moose blocked somebody, he stayed blocked. When the Moose was called on to open a hole in the line for one of the Bears' runners, the hole more often than not resembled an open garage door.

Now in his senior season, the Moose had twice been named to the all-conference team and was considered a cinch for all-state. He spent a lot of his spare time, when he wasn't in a classroom or on the football field, reading letters from colleges eager to have the Moose pursue higher education —and football—at their institution.

But the Moose had a hang-up.

He didn't go public with his hang-up until the sixth game of the season. But, looking back, most of his teammates agreed that probably the Moose had been nurturing the hang-up secretly for two years or more.

The Moose wanted to carry the ball.

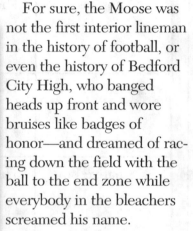

For sure, the Moose was not the first interior lineman in the history of football, or even the history of Bedford City High, who banged heads up front and wore bruises like badges of honor—and dreamed of racing down the field with the ball to the end zone while everybody in the bleachers screamed his name.

But most linemen, it seems, are able to stifle the urge. The idea may pop into their minds from time to time, but in their hearts they know they can't run fast enough, they know they can't do that fancy dancing to elude tacklers, they know they aren't trained to read blocks. They know that their strengths and talents are best utilized in the line. Football is, after all, a team sport, and everyone plays the position where he most helps the team. And so these linemen, or most of them, go back to banging heads without saying the first word about the dream that flickered through their minds.

Not so with the Moose.

That sixth game, when the Moose's hang-up first came into public view, had ended with the

Moose truly in all his glory as the Bears' left tackle. Yes, glory—but uncheered and sort of anonymous. The Bears were trailing 21–17 and had the ball on Mitchell High's five-yard line, fourth down, with time running out. The rule in such a situation is simple—the best back carries the ball behind the best blocker—and it is a rule seldom violated by those in control of their faculties. The Bears, of course, followed the rule. That meant Jerry Dixon running behind the Moose's blocking. With the snap of the ball, the Moose knocked down one lineman, bumped another one aside, and charged forward to flatten an approaching linebacker. Jerry did a little jig behind the Moose and then ran into the end zone, virtually untouched, to win the game.

After circling in the end zone a moment while the cheers echoed through the night, Jerry did run across and hug the Moose, that's true. Jerry knew who had made the touchdown possible.

But it wasn't the Moose's name that everybody was shouting. The fans in the bleachers were cheering Jerry Dixon.

It was probably at that precise moment that the Moose decided to go public.

In the dressing room, Coach Buford Williams was making his rounds among the cheering players and came to a halt in front of the Moose. "It was your great blocking that did it," he said.

"I want to carry the ball," the Moose said.

Coach Williams was already turning away and taking a step toward the next player due an accolade when his brain registered the fact that the Moose had said something strange. He was expecting the Moose to say, "Aw, gee, thanks, Coach." That was what the Moose always said when the coach issued a compliment. But the Moose had said something else. The coach turned back to the Moose, a look of disbelief on his face. "What did you say?"

"I want to carry the ball."

Coach Williams was good at quick recoveries, as any high school football coach had better be. He gave a tolerant smile and a little nod and said, "You keep right on blocking, son."

This time Coach Williams made good on his turn and moved away from the Moose.

The following week's practice and the next Friday's game passed without further incident. After all, the game was a road game over at Cartwright High, thirty-five miles away. The Moose wanted to carry the ball in front of the Bedford City fans.

Then the Moose went to work.

He caught up with the coach on the way to the practice field on Wednesday. "Remember," he said, leaning forward and down a little to get his face in the coach's face, "I said I want to carry the ball."

Coach Williams must have been thinking about something else because it took him a minute to look up into the Moose's face, and even then he didn't say anything.

"I meant it," the Moose said.

"Meant what?"

"I want to run the ball."

"Oh," Coach Williams said. Yes, he remembered. "Son, you're a great left tackle, a great blocker. Let's leave it that way."

The Moose let the remaining days of the practice week and then the game on Friday night against Edgewood High pass while he reviewed strategies. The review led him to Dan Blevins, the Bears' quarterback. If the signal-caller would join in, maybe Coach Williams would listen.

"Yeah, I heard," Dan said. "But, look, what about Joe Wright at guard, Bill Slocum at right tackle, even Herbie Watson at center. They might all want to carry the ball. What are we going to do—take turns? It doesn't work that way."

So much for Dan Blevins.

The Moose found that most of the players in the backfield agreed with Dan. They couldn't see any reason why the Moose should carry the ball, especially in place of themselves. Even Jerry Dixon, who owed a lot of his glory to the Moose's blocking, gaped in disbelief at the Moose's idea. The Moose, however, got some support from his fellow linemen. Maybe they had dreams of their own, and saw value in a precedent.

As the days went by, the word spread—not just on the practice field and in the corridors of Bedford City High, but all around town. The players by now were openly taking sides. Some thought it a jolly good idea that the Moose carry the ball. Others, like Dan Blevins, held to the purist line—a left tackle plays left tackle, a ball-carrier carries the ball, and that's it.

Around town, the vote wasn't even close. Everyone wanted the Moose to carry the ball.

"Look, son," Coach Williams said to the Moose on the practice field the Thursday before the Benton Heights game, "this has gone far enough. Fun is fun. A joke is a joke. But let's drop it."

"Just once," the Moose pleaded.

Coach Williams looked at the Moose and didn't answer.

The Moose didn't know what that meant.

The Benton Heights Tigers were duck soup for the Bears, as everyone knew they would be. The Bears scored in their first three possessions and led 28–0 at the half. The hapless Tigers had yet to cross the fifty-yard line under their own steam.

All the Bears, of course, were enjoying the way the game was going, as were the Bedford City fans jamming the bleachers.

Coach Williams looked irritated when the crowd on a couple of occasions broke into a chant: "Give the Moose the ball! Give the Moose the ball!"

On the field, the Moose did not know whether to grin at hearing his name shouted by the crowd or to frown because the sound of his name was irritating the coach. Was the crowd going to talk Coach Williams into putting the Moose in the backfield? Probably not; Coach Williams didn't bow to that kind of pressure. Was the coach going to refuse to give the ball to the Moose just to show the crowd—and the Moose and the rest of the players—who was boss? The Moose feared so.

In his time on the sideline, when the defensive unit was on the field, the Moose, of course, said nothing to Coach Williams. He knew better than to break the coach's concentration during a game—even a runaway victory—with a comment on any subject at all, much less his desire to carry the ball. As a matter of fact, the Moose was careful to stay out of the coach's line of vision, especially when the crowd was chanting "Give the Moose the ball!"

By the end of the third quarter the Bears were leading 42–0.

Coach Williams had been feeding substitutes into the game since halftime, but the Bears kept marching on. And now, in the opening minutes of the fourth quarter, the Moose and his teammates were standing on the Tigers' five-yard line, about to pile on another touchdown.

The Moose saw his substitute, Larry Hinden, getting a slap on the behind and then running onto the field. The Moose turned to leave.

Then he heard Larry tell the referee, "Hinden for Holbrook."

Holbrook? Chad Holbrook, the fullback?

Chad gave the coach a funny look and jogged off the field.

Larry joined the huddle and said, "Coach says the Moose at fullback and give him the ball."

Dan Blevins said, "Really?"

"Really."

The Moose was giving his grin—"sweet," some of the teachers called it; "nice," others said.

"I want to do an end run," the Moose said.

Dan looked at the sky a moment, then said, "What does it matter?"

The quarterback took the snap from center, moved back and to his right while turning, and extended the ball to the Moose.

The Moose took the ball and cradled it in his right hand. So far, so good. He hadn't fumbled. Probably both Coach Williams and Dan were surprised.

He ran a couple of steps and looked out in front and said aloud, "Whoa!"

Where had all those tacklers come from?

The whole world seemed to be peopled with players in red jerseys—the red of the Benton Heights Tigers. They all were looking straight at the Moose and advancing toward him. They looked very determined, and not friendly at all. And there were so many of them. The Moose had faced tough guys in the line, but usually one at a time, or maybe two. But this—five or six. And all of them heading for him.

The Moose screeched to a halt, whirled, and ran the other way.

Dan Blevins blocked somebody in a red jersey breaking through the middle of the line, and the Moose wanted to stop running and thank him. But he kept going.

His reverse had caught the Tigers' defenders going the wrong way, and the field in front of the Moose looked open. But his blockers were going the wrong way, too. Maybe that was why the field looked so open. What did it matter, though, with the field clear in front of him? This was going to be a cakewalk; the Moose was going to score a touchdown.

Then, again—"Whoa!"

Players with red jerseys were beginning to fill the empty space—a lot of them. And they were all running toward the Moose. They were kind of low, with their arms spread, as if they wanted to hit him hard and then grab him.

A picture of Jerry Dixon dancing his little jig and wriggling between tacklers flashed through the Moose's mind. How did Jerry do that? Well, no time to ponder that one right now.

The Moose lowered his shoulder and thundered ahead, into the cloud of red jerseys. Something hit his left thigh. It hurt. Then something pounded his hip, then his shoulder. They both hurt. Somebody was hanging on to him and was a terrible drag. How could he run with somebody hanging on to him? He knew he was going down, but maybe he was across the goal. He hit the ground hard, with somebody coming down on top of him, right on the small of his back.

The Moose couldn't move. They had him pinned. Wasn't the referee supposed to get these guys off?

Finally the load was gone and the Moose, still holding the ball, got to his knees and one hand, then stood.

He heard the screaming of the crowd, and he saw the scoreboard blinking.

He had scored.

His teammates were slapping him on the shoulder pads and laughing and shouting.

The Moose grinned, but he had a strange and distant look in his eyes.

He jogged to the sideline, the roars of the crowd still ringing in his ears.

"Okay, son?" Coach Williams asked.

The Moose was puffing. He took a couple of deep breaths. He relived for a moment the first sight of a half dozen players in red jerseys, all with one target—him. He saw again the menacing horde of red jerseys that had risen up just when he'd thought he had clear sailing to the goal. They all zeroed in on him, the Moose, alone.

The Moose glanced at the coach, took another deep breath, and said, "Never again."

A Meaningful Word

The word *anonymous* is used in the story to describe how the Moose feels during a successful game. The writer says that the Moose was "truly in all his glory as the Bears' left tackle. Yes, glory—but uncheered and sort of anonymous." Learning the meaning of this word will help you understand the Moose and his actions.

Directions: The word *anonymous* can have two definitions: a) not named or identified; b) lacking individuality. Use these definitions to answer the questions that follow.

1. What is it about the Moose that makes him anonymous?

   _____

   _____

   _____

   _____

2. What is it about being a lineman that makes a person anonymous?

   _____

   _____

   _____

3. According to the Moose, what would be the opposite of anonymous? Explain.

   _____

   _____

4. Do you think the Moose enjoys his brief time not being anonymous? Explain.

   _____

   _____

   _____

5. Do you think that the Moose discovers any benefits to being anonymous? Explain.

   _____

   _____

   _____

Two Visions

In the story "Just Once," the Moose and his coach view the Moose's goal differently. This difference leads to the main conflict in the story.

Directions: The chart below contains four questions that relate to the Moose and his coach. Write your responses in the space provided to the right of each question. The fifth question asks for your opinion about the decision to let the Moose carry the ball.

1. What is the Moose's goal?	
2. What do you think the Moose hopes to gain by achieving his goal?	
3. How does the coach view the Moose's goal?	
4. How does the coach think his team will be affected if the Moose gets what he wants?	
5. Do you think the coach made the right decision when he allowed the Moose to carry the ball? Explain your response.	

Hard Lessons

Directions: Moose learns a lot about himself and his teammates by carrying the ball "just once." Read each passage below, and describe what the Moose learns during each moment described.

Passage	Lesson
1. "Dan Blevins blocked somebody in a red jersey breaking through the middle of the line, and the Moose wanted to stop running and thank him. But he kept going."	
2. "A picture of Jerry Dixon dancing his little jig and wriggling between tacklers flashed through the Moose's mind. How did Jerry do that? Well, no time to ponder that one right now."	
3. "The Moose lowered his shoulder and thundered ahead, into the cloud of red jerseys. Something hit his left thigh. It hurt. Then something pounded his hip, then his shoulder. They both hurt. Somebody was hanging on to him and was a terrible drag."	

Your Turn

The Moose learns a great deal about himself by running with the ball. Describe a similar event in your life when you learned about your limits.

TEST

by Theodore L. Thomas

As You Read: Decide whether Robert is a good driver or not.

Robert Proctor was a good driver for so young a man. The Turnpike curved gently ahead of him, lightly traveled on this cool morning in May. He felt relaxed and alert. Two hours of driving had not yet produced the twinges of fatigue that appeared first in the muscles in the base of the neck. The sun was bright, but not glaring, and the air smelled fresh and clean. He breathed it deeply, and blew it out noisily. It was a good day for driving.

He glanced quickly at the slim, grey-haired woman sitting in the front seat with him. Her mouth was curved in a quiet smile. She watched the trees and the fields slip by on her side of the pike. Robert Proctor immediately looked back at the road. He said, "Enjoying it, Mom?"

"Yes, Robert." Her voice was as cool as the morning. "It is very pleasant to sit here. I was thinking of the driving I did for you when you were little. I wonder if you enjoyed it as much as I enjoy this."

He smiled, embarrassed. "Sure I did."

She reached over and patted him gently on the arm, and then turned back to the scenery.

He listened to the smooth purr of the engine. Up ahead he saw a great truck, spouting a geyser of smoke as it sped along the Turnpike. Behind it, not passing it, was a long blue convertible, content to drive in the wake of the truck. Robert Proctor noted the arrangement and filed it in the back of his mind. He was slowly overtaking them, but he would not reach them for another minute or two.

He listened to the purr of the engine, and he was pleased with the sound. He had tuned that engine himself over the objections of the mechanic. The engine idled rough now, but it ran smoothly at high speed. You needed a special feel to do good work on engines, and Robert Proctor knew he had it. No one in the world had a feel like his for the tune of an engine.

It was a good morning for driving, and his mind was filled with good thoughts. He pulled nearly abreast of the blue convertible and began to pass it. His speed was a few miles per hour above the Turnpike limit, but his car was under perfect control. The blue convertible suddenly swung out from behind the truck. It swung out without warning and struck his car near the right front fender, knocking his car to the shoulder on the left side of the Turnpike lane.

Robert Proctor was a good driver, too wise to slam on the brakes. He fought the steering wheel to hold the car on a straight path. The left wheels sank into the soft left shoulder, and the car tugged to pull to the left and cross the island and enter the lanes carrying the cars heading in the opposite direction. He held it, then the wheel struck a rock buried in the soft dirt, and the left front tire blew out. The car slewed, and it was then that his mother began to scream.

The car turned sideways and skidded part of the way out into the other lanes. Robert Proctor fought against the steering wheel to straighten the car, but the drag of the blown tire was too much. The scream rang steadily in his ears, and even as he strained at the wheel one part of his mind wondered coolly how a scream could so long be sustained without a breath. An oncoming car struck his radiator from the side and spun him viciously, full into the left-hand lanes.

He was flung into his mother's lap, and she was thrown against the right door. It held. With his left hand he reached for the steering wheel and pulled himself erect against the force of the spin. He turned the wheel to the left, and tried to stop the spin and career out of the lanes of oncoming traffic. His mother was unable to right herself; she lay against the door, her cry rising and falling with the eccentric spin of the car.

The car lost some of its momentum. During one of the spins he twisted the wheel straight, and the car wobblingly stopped spinning and headed down the lane. Before Robert Proctor could turn it off the pike to safety a car loomed ahead of him, bearing down on him. There was a man at the wheel of that other car, sitting rigid, unable to move, eyes wide and staring and filled with fright. Alongside the man was a girl, her head against the back of the seat, soft curls framing a lovely face, her eyes closed in easy sleep. It was not the fear in the man that reached into Robert Proctor; it was the trusting helplessness in the face of the sleeping girl. The two cars sped closer to each other, and Robert Proctor could not change the direction of his

car. The driver of the other car remained frozen at the wheel. At the last moment Robert Proctor sat motionless staring into the face of the onrushing, sleeping girl, his mother's cry still sounding in his ears. He heard no crash when the two cars collided head-on at a high rate of speed. He felt something push into his stomach, and the world began to go grey. Just before he lost consciousness he heard the scream stop, and he knew then that he had been hearing a single, short-lived scream that had only seemed to drag on and on. There came a painless wrench, and then darkness.

Robert Proctor seemed to be at the bottom of a deep black well. There was a spot of faint light in the far distance, and he could hear the rumble of a distant voice. He tried to pull himself toward the light and the sound, but the effort was too great. He lay still and gathered himself and tried again. The light grew brighter and the voice louder. He tried harder, again, and he

drew closer. Then he opened his eyes full and looked at the man sitting in front of him.

"You all right, Son?" asked the man. He wore a blue uniform, and his round, beefy face was familiar.

Robert Proctor tentatively moved his head, and discovered he was seated in a reclining chair, unharmed, and able to move his arms and legs with no trouble. He looked around the room, and he remembered.

The man in the uniform saw the growing intelligence in his eyes and he said, "No harm done, Son. You just took the last part of your driver's test."

Robert Proctor focused his eyes on the man. Though he saw the man clearly, he seemed to see the faint face of the sleeping girl in front of him.

The uniformed man continued to speak. "We put you through an accident under hypnosis—do it to everybody these days before they can get their driver's licenses. Makes better drivers of them, more careful drivers the rest of their lives. Remember it now? Coming in here and all?"

Robert Proctor nodded, thinking of the sleeping girl. She never would have awakened; she would have passed right from a sweet, temporary sleep into the dark heavy sleep of death, nothing in between. His mother would have been bad enough; after all, she was pretty old. The sleeping girl was downright waste.

The uniformed man was still speaking. "So you're all set now. You pay me the ten dollar fee, and sign this application, and we'll have your license in the mail in a day or two." He did not look up.

Robert Proctor placed a ten dollar bill on the table in front of him, glanced over the application and signed it. He looked up to find two white-uniformed men, standing one on each side of him, and he frowned in annoyance. He started to speak, but the uniformed man spoke first. "Sorry, Son. You failed. You're sick; you need treatment."

The two men lifted Robert Proctor to his feet, and he said, "Take your hands off me. What is this?"

The uniformed man said, "Nobody should want to drive a car after going through what you just went through. It should take months before you can even think of driving again, but you're ready right now. Killing people doesn't bother you. We don't let your kind run around loose in society any more. But don't you worry now, Son. They'll take good care of you, and they'll fix you up." He nodded to the two men, and they began to march Robert Proctor out.

At the door he spoke, and his voice was so urgent the two men paused. Robert Proctor said, "You can't really mean this. I'm still dreaming, aren't I? This is still part of the test, isn't it?"

The uniformed man said, "*How do any of us know?*" And they dragged Robert Proctor out the door, knees stiff, feet dragging, his rubber heels sliding along the two grooves worn into the floor.

Chain of Events

A *sequence*, or chain of events, makes up a story's plot. Recognizing the sequence is essential to understanding the meaning of a story.

Directions: Number the following events from 1 to 8, with *1* being the first event and 8 the last. Then answer the questions about the plot that follow.

_____ Robert places $10 on a table and signs an application for a license.

_____ Robert's car collides with a car carrying a sleeping girl.

_____ Two men in white uniforms approach Robert, and he's told that he's failed the test.

_____ Robert is surrounded by darkness and feels like he's at the bottom of a deep well.

_____ A blue convertible pulls out in front of Robert's car and hits it.

_____ Robert and his mother are enjoying a pleasant ride.

_____ A man in a blue uniform explains to Robert that he has experienced an accident under hypnosis.

_____ Robert begins to pass a blue convertible.

1. When did you first suspect that Robert was not in a true car accident? Circle the incident in the list above.

2. What would Robert have to do to pass the test?

_____

_____

_____

_____

Analyzing Mood

Mood is the emotional response the reader has to a story. For example, a story might make the reader feel happy, nervous, or angry. The story "Test" contains several moods. Like Robert, readers are taken on a ride and jolted from one mood to another.

Directions: As you read the following passages from the story, decide what overall mood is created by the passage and complete each sentence that follows. Then <u>underline</u> the words or phrases that help create that mood.

1. "Robert Proctor was a good driver for so young a man. The Turnpike curved gently ahead of him, lightly traveled on this cool morning in May. He felt relaxed and alert. Two hours of driving had not yet produced the twinges of fatigue that appeared first in the muscles in the base of the neck. The sun was bright, but not glaring, and the air smelled fresh and clean. He breathed it deeply, and blew it out noisily. It was a good day for driving."

   The passage makes me feel _____

   _____

2. "At the last moment Robert Proctor sat motionless staring into the face of the onrushing, sleeping girl, his mother's cry still sounding in his ears. He heard no crash when the two cars collided head-on at a high rate of speed. He felt something push into his stomach, and the world began to go grey. Just before he lost consciousness he heard the scream stop, and he knew then that he had been hearing a single, short-lived scream that had only seemed to drag on and on. There came a painless wrench, and then darkness."

   The passage makes me feel _____

   _____

3. "The uniformed man said, 'Nobody should want to drive a car after going through what you just went through. It should take months before you can even think of driving again, but you're ready right now. Killing people doesn't bother you. We don't let your kind run around loose in society any more. But don't you worry now, Son. They'll take good care of you, and they'll fix you up.' He nodded to the two men, and they began to march Robert Proctor out."

   The passage makes me feel _____

   _____

Interpreting the Meaning

Authors don't provide everything needed to understand a story. They know that readers bring their own experiences and attitudes with them as they read. Authors allow, and even expect, readers to interpret. *Interpreting* means using your own experience and understanding of the story to draw conclusions.

Directions: Answer each of the following questions by using your knowledge of the story.

1. Do you think the test Robert Proctor took was fair?

   Ⓐ yes   Ⓑ no

   Explain your opinion below.

   _____

   _____

   _____

   _____

2. Do you think Robert would make a good driver?

   Ⓐ yes   Ⓑ no

   Give reasons for your response.

   _____

   _____

   _____

   _____

3. Interpret the title of the story.

   I think the title of the story means

   _____

   _____

   _____

   _____

Reading Myths and Folktales

Myths and folktales both entertain and instruct. They both contain events and characters that appeal to our imaginations. And both folktales and myths were told orally long before they were written down. However, there are differences between the two types of stories.

Myths are often about gods and heroes. Myths might focus on the actions of the gods or the ways gods and humans interact. And myths explore questions about nature and human experience. For example, a myth might explain why there are different seasons or why human suffering exists.

Folktales, on the other hand, are likely to be about animals that talk and act like people. These characters often teach important lessons or morals. For example, they might show how a poor person can use his wits to succeed or the importance of working together.

The most important thing about folktales and myths is that they are both fun to read!

TIPS FOR READING MYTHS AND FOLKTALES

As you read, pay attention to these three features.

1) **Characters**
   If the characters are gods and heroes, you're probably reading a myth. If they're ordinary people or talking animals, you're more likely to be reading a folktale.

2) **Events**
   The events in myths often describe the actions of the gods and the way gods and humans interact. Events in folktales often describe a fanciful situation or the relationships between animals.

3) **Lessons**
   Myths often explain nature or answer important human questions, such as how evil came into the world. Folktales, on the other hand, teach morals or lessons.

THE GODDESS AND THE WEAVER

a tale from ancient Greece
retold by Cynthia M. Martin

As you read: Write your thoughts in the Think-Along column on the right.

Story

Think-Along

The immortal gods of Olympus did more than sip nectar, eat ambrosia, and listen to the Muses play sweetly on their golden harps. The Olympians had their own interests. And each was a patron of earthly creatures or even an activity. For example, Poseidon, the mighty god of the sea, also protected and trained horses. Hera, the queen of all the gods, was the patroness of women and helped out in marriages and childbirth. Hermes, the gods' messenger, was the patron of thieves and the inventor of the lyre, a stringed instrument. Finally, Athena, the goddess of wisdom, was the patron of arts and crafts, especially of spinning and weaving. And in her opinion, that made her the greatest weaver in the universe—which brings us to our story.

One day Athena decided to go down to Earth to visit her favorite city. That would be the city named after her, Athens. "I'd better disguise myself," she said to herself before she left for her journey. "After all, I don't want to blind the humans with my glory." So instead of wearing her usual shining armor and precious jewels, Athena dressed herself in a plain gown and a dark cloak. "There," she said, satisfied. "Now I look like a mortal."

For a god, travel is no problem at all. Athena simply imagined Athens, and suddenly there she was, standing in front of the great gates that led into the city.

The goddess joined the stream of people making their way into Athens. It was festival day, and the great marketplace was full of merchants exhibiting their goods. Athena wandered freely from one booth to the other. She bought a cup of cool juice from one merchant. The fragrant liquid quenched her thirst nicely.

Not as fine as the gods' nectar, she thought, but quite tasty for a human concoction.

Next she examined some of the pins and rings on display. "Not nearly as fine as the jewels crafted by Hephaestus, the gods' craftsman," she murmured to herself. "Of course, no

human can create anything as beautiful as the work of a god."

Athena kept walking through the city, blending in with the crowds as she went. She enjoyed listening to the humans chatter about their everyday concerns. She noticed two women were standing near a fountain, talking excitedly. Athena made her way toward them, just in time to hear the older woman exclaim to the other, "Oh my dear, you must go see her. Why, I've never seen anything like it in my life. Her work is as beautiful as the goddess Athena's!"

Athena stiffened. As beautiful as my work? I'll be the judge of that, she thought. She touched the woman on the sleeve.

"Excuse me," she said sweetly. "I couldn't help but overhear. Please, tell me more. Who is this wonderful craftsperson?"

"The weaver Arachne," the woman replied. "She has a shop just on the other side of the square. Her tapestries are absolutely exquisite."

Athena's heart went cold with rage. *She* had invented the loom, and she alone wove cloaks for Zeus, the king of the gods. How could any human claim to weave so well?

"Thank you," she said. "I will certainly visit her." She nodded to the women and walked away.

Athena crossed the square and found a row of small shops. Above one hung a sign that read "Weaver." She pushed open the door and stepped inside. Against one wall stood an enormous loom covered with an expanse of misty fabric. Athena caught her breath. The cloth was woven in a dazzling rainbow of color! It was the most intricate and beautiful tapestry she had ever seen done by a human. Could it possibly be as lovely as my own work? she asked herself.

A young woman sat on the stool in front of the tapestry. She glanced up as Athena came in, but her shuttle kept moving on the loom.

"May I help you?" she asked, returning her attention to her work.

"Are you Arachne, the weaver?" the goddess asked.

"Yes, I am," Arachne answered. "Are you interested in my tapestries?"

"You might say that," Athena replied coldly. And with a wave of her hand, her human disguise dropped away. Athena's radiance filled the room like the sparkle of a giant diamond. Suddenly weak with fear, Arachne slid off her stool and knelt on the floor.

"Who . . . who are you?" she stammered.

"I am Athena, goddess of wisdom *and* the inventor of the loom," the goddess declared. "I hear you're quite a weaver, my dear. In fact, I'm told that your fabrics are fine enough to be displayed on Mt. Olympus!"

Arachne swallowed hard. She kept her eyes on the floor, but her voice was firm as she spoke. "Great goddess, pray, do not listen to gossips in the marketplace. It is true that I am proud of my work, but never have I compared it with yours."

"That makes no difference!" Athena cried. "Other people are comparing it, and I won't stand for it! From this day forward, I forbid you to weave again."

Arachne jumped to her feet. "That's unfair!" she cried, forgetting herself for a moment. "I am a weaver. It's the only craft I know, and I love it more than anything in the world! How can you condemn me to misery to satisfy your own pride? Is that justice, mighty goddess of wisdom?"

Athena thought for a moment. "I admire your devotion to your craft," she said, "so I propose a contest in the marketplace. Each of us will weave a tapestry. The people will judge whose is the finest. If you win, you may continue to weave. If I win, you must never touch a loom again."

Arachne hesitated. Challenge a goddess? She had heard what happened to mortals who defied the gods. But this was her only chance to save her beloved craft. "Agreed," she replied.

"Very well," Athena nodded. "Until tomorrow." With that she vanished.

By the next day, everyone had heard about the contest between the goddess and the weaver. When the two women arrived, the marketplace was overflowing with spectators. Two looms were placed in the middle of the square. Each was surrounded with baskets of yarn and threads of every possible color. Athena seated herself in front of her loom and looked over at Arachne. The girl appeared pale and tired but her hands were steady on the loom.

"Let us begin," Athena said.

The two weavers started their work. Their shuttles flew in and out of the loom like graceful birds. Athena wove a tapestry of brilliant colors, interlaced with gold and silver

threads. In a short time, her fabric displayed a pattern of flowers so realistic that the bystanders could actually smell their perfume. When she finished, she held up her work for all to see. The crowd cheered wildly. Athena sat down again, flushed with satisfaction. She glanced over at Arachne.

"And how have you done, my dear?" she asked.

Arachne arose from her stool and bowed. "I will let the people decide," she said.

Everyone crowded close to see Arachne's fabric. It was filled with dazzling birds, each one so real that the people could hear its song echoing in the air. The crowd was silent for a moment, then one of them came and bowed before Athena.

"Great goddess," he said "your work is breathtaking; no one would deny that. However, Arachne's work is every bit as fine. We are unable to choose a winner."

Athena stood up, her face filled with rage. She strode over to Arachne's loom and waved her hand. The loom and the tapestry burst into flames. In a moment, all that remained was a pile of ashes. Then she turned to Arachne.

"You love to weave," Athena said. "You love it enough that you dare to humiliate a goddess. However, I swore that if I did not win, you could continue to weave. But you agreed that if you did not win, you would never touch a loom again. So be it."

The goddess waved her hand. Arachne's hair dropped off. Then her nose and ears vanished. Her arms and legs multiplied. Arachne looked down in horror and saw her whole body shrink in size until she was no larger than a marble.

"Look!" cried one of the bystanders. "That horrid little creature there! What is it?"

Athena smiled. "A spider," she replied. "Mortals, let that be a lesson to you. Never defy the gods!"

As the crowd watched, the spider headed across the square and into the nearest tree. Immediately it began to weave an exquisite web between two branches.

Today, Arachne's daughters still practice their weaving wherever they go. And their exquisite tapestries remind mortals to think twice before they challenge the gods!

Comprehending Plot

Ancient storytellers often made up stories to explain events in nature. This story, for example, explains why spiders weave beautiful webs—the goddess Athena was jealous of Arachne's skills and turned her into a spider.

But this isn't the whole story. Several minor events lead up to the final ending. And each minor event occurs for a reason. All of these reasons and events make up the *plot*, or storyline.

Directions: Supply a reason for each event in the plot of "The Goddess and the Weaver."

Event	Reason
1. Athena goes to Athens disguised as a mortal.	
2. Athena is filled with anger in the marketplace.	
3. Athena goes to Arachne's shop.	
4. Athena removes her disguise.	
5. Athena demands that Arachne never weave again.	
6. Arachne questions the fairness of Athena's demand.	
7. Athena challenges Arachne to a contest of skills.	
8. Athena burns Arachne's tapestry and loom.	
9. Athena turns Arachne into a spider.	
10. Spiders, or *arachnids*, weave beautiful webs today.	

Has Justice Been Served?

According to the dictionary, *justice* is giving someone the reward or punishment he or she deserves. In this story, Arachne asks the goddess Athena, "How can you condemn me to misery to satisfy your own pride? Is that justice?" This activity will help you decide the answer to Arachne's question.

Directions: Answer the following questions about "The Goddess and the Weaver."

1. Why does Athena demand that Arachne never weave again? _____

_____

2. Do you think Athena is right to demand that Arachne never weave again? Ⓐ yes   Ⓑ no
Give reasons for your opinion. _____

_____

3. In your opinion, is Arachne justified in standing up to Athena? Ⓐ yes   Ⓑ no
Give reasons for your opinion. _____

_____

4. What are the terms of the agreement Athena offers Arachne?

_____

_____

5. Do you think these terms are fair to Arachne? Ⓐ yes   Ⓑ no
Give reasons for your opinion. _____

_____

6. Read the last section again from the point where the member of the crowd tells Athena that the tapestries are equal. Explain how Athena upholds her end of the bargain with Arachne. _____

_____

THE SNAKE AND THE PRINCESS

Prereading: No Ordinary Tale

You've encountered princes and princesses in many tales, but you've probably never met any quite like Ntombinde and the Snake Prince. This exercise will help you prepare to read about these characters.

Directions: Answer the questions in the left-hand column before reading the story. Then answer the questions in the right-hand column after reading it.

Before Reading	After Reading
1. What words would you use to describe the typical princess?	Describe the character of Ntombinde.
2. What words would you use to describe the typical prince?	Describe the Snake Prince.
3. How do a prince and a princess usually meet? (Who pursues whom?)	How do Ntombinde and the Snake Prince meet?
4. How do such stories usually end?	How does Ntombinde respond to the marriage proposal?

THE SNAKE AND THE PRINCESS

A tale from the Congo
retold by Eleanora E. Tate

As you read: Think about how Ntombinde compares to other princesses.

In some ways, Ntombinde was an ordinary princess. She behaved just as you would expect a princess to behave. She was compassionate and caring. And she always thought of others before herself.

But in other ways, Ntombinde was a very extraordinary princess. For example, she was very curious. She often went exploring by herself, just to see how other people lived. But most of all, Ntombinde was very courageous. Once she fought off a band of thieves who were pillaging the countryside. Another time she challenged a river monster to a fight and triumphed.

Now the king was proud of his daughter. Yet he was embarrassed by her as well.

One day the king spoke to his wife about Ntombinde. "Where's her modesty?" he asked. "How will we ever find someone to marry her? She's just too outspoken. She must get that from you."

"I think that whoever becomes Ntombinde's lover will be a lucky man," the queen said with a playful smile. "For a *real* man, our daughter's courage and outspokenness will not be a threat.

Who knows, Ntombinde may even save a man's life."

That spring Ntombinde was invited to a wedding many kingdoms away. As always, she traveled alone.

But along the way, night fell with Ntombinde far from her destination. As luck would have it, she came upon a small kingdom. She learned that it was ruled by Queen Manyoka— widow of the late king. Ntombinde asked the queen for lodging at the royal palace.

Queen Manyoka graciously took her in and led her to a beautifully decorated room.

"Before I leave you, I must tell you the story of this room," the queen said. "Then you can decide if you wish to stay in it."

"I'm ready to listen," replied Ntombinde with enthusiasm. This sounded like an adventure and, as you know, Ntombinde loved adventure!

"Long ago, the king and I lived in happiness with our family," began the queen. "We had four children. Besides our eldest son, we had two younger sons and a daughter.

"Then controversy set in," continued the queen sadly. "The younger children thought it unfair that their oldest brother was to inherit the throne.

"Now our younger children were spiteful and lazy. On the other hand, our elder son was hardworking, intelligent, and caring. Little wonder he became our favorite child.

"We tried to keep the younger children happy. We even increased their inheritance. But as time went on, the three youngest became more and more jealous.

"Finally they paid an evil sorcerer to get rid of their innocent brother. The sorcerer cast a spell that changed our beloved son into a snake."

The queen paused. With difficulty she finished her story. "The jealous action of our youngest children broke the king's heart. Finally he died of grief.

"The sad thing is, the young ones regretted their action. They were horrified by the sorcerer's power. Unfortunately they could do nothing to break the spell.

"We have since found out that only a maiden pure in heart can change my son back into a man."

"Have many women tried to save your son?" asked Ntombinde.

"Many have tried," Queen Manyoka replied. "But they only wanted our son's riches. He sensed their greed, and his snake heart hardened. He killed them all."

Queen Manyoka looked into Ntombinde's eyes. "Now do you still want to spend the night here?" she asked quietly.

"Yes," was Ntombinde's immediate reply. "I am curious to meet your son."

With that, the queen ordered a huge meal of meat and palm juice put on the table. Then she opened a window in the room. "Each night he returns to eat," she explained. "Perhaps you will

be the one to bring a change of heart in my Snake Prince. Nothing else—not even the gods—can do it."

With these words, the queen turned and left the room.

Now common sense warned Ntombinde not to sleep near an open window. And she certainly didn't want to be surprised by a large snake. So she vowed to stay awake all night.

When daylight came, Ntombinde was still awake. The food was still there. But outside the window she found a patch of gold and black snakeskin.

"My son has been here," Manyoka said when she saw the skin. "And he didn't bother you. That's a good sign. Will you stay another night?"

The courageous Ntombinde agreed. Again Manyoka set out food and again Ntombinde stayed awake. In the morning the food remained uneaten. But this time servants found two patches of snakeskin outside.

"I think he's studying you," said Manyoka.

"I'm studying him too," said Ntombinde.

Manyoka asked Ntombinde to stay one more night. And now the younger sons and daughter begged her to stay too.

"You who made him suffer so now wish for his return?" Ntombinde asked with surprise. "Do you plan to give him yet more pain?"

"Oh no. All of this is our fault," admitted one brother.

"It was all so long ago," added the daughter. "We were selfish fools. Our tutors said we had the hardest heads in the whole kingdom."

"We were too busy listening to the gods of greed to learn anything," said the other brother. "And too lazy. We raced horses all day and danced all night. Now your courage is our only hope of bringing our brother back."

On this third night Ntombinde pretended to be asleep. Finally around midnight she heard a noise outside. Through half-closed eyes she saw a huge serpent glide in through the window. The Snake Prince coiled his golden-black body and lifted his head. Then he stared into Ntombinde's face.

The snake's face was that of a handsome man. Ntombinde had never seen such a sad face. Her heart melted as she fell in love with the Snake Prince.

But then the snake spoke. His face twisted into a mask of evil. "Why are you here?" he hissed harshly.

"Because you've already suffered more than most men ever will," Ntombinde replied. "And because your sadness touches my heart."

"You lie!" spat the snake. "You're just like all the rest. You hope to become my bride. And you want to be queen of this land so that you can get your hands on my riches."

"I don't need your riches," Ntombinde replied with fire in her eyes. "I'm already rich. I'm compassionate, curious, and courageous. And I'm not afraid to speak my mind."

"You lie. You're conniving and greedy." The snake towered over her. "I hate my brothers and sister for what they did to me. I hate everyone. First I'll kill you with my venom. Then I'll devour you."

The snake opened his mouth, showing his huge fangs. But Ntombinde stood her ground.

"Stop that!" Ntombinde said sternly. "In your heart you're still a man. But your heart has been poisoned by the hate of a snake. The ways of a snake cannot live in the heart of a man."

The snake was surprised by the young woman's outburst. He closed his mouth and stared at her in wonder.

But Ntombinde had just begun. "Devour me?" she laughed. "You do, and I'll give you a stomachache you won't forget. And if you call me a liar again, I'll stomp on your tail."

The Snake Prince pulled in his tail and backed away. "You're not big enough for a meal anyway," the snake said sullenly.

Still watching her, the snake slithered to the table and began to eat. Ntombinde thought she saw a smile dance briefly around the serpent's mouth.

Slowly Ntombinde approached the table. As if in a trance, the Snake Prince froze. Then without warning, the young princess gently kissed the prince on his snakeskin cheek.

The Snake Prince let out a deep sigh. The prince's human spirit broke through the snake's hateful hold on his heart. The snakeskin fell away.

Before Ntombinde stood a tall, handsome, ebony-skinned man wrapped in golden robes. The grateful prince immediately asked Ntombinde to marry him.

Ntombinde just smiled. "Let me see what my father has to say first."

Determining Word Meanings

The first step in figuring out the meaning of a new word is deciding on what method you will use. You can determine word meaning by using **context clues,** looking for recognizable **word parts** or by **using a dictionary.**

Directions: Read each passage below. Decide which of the methods described above is the best way to learn the meaning of the **bold-faced** word. Write **C** for context clues, **W** for word parts, or **D** for dictionary. Then use the method you've selected to determine the definition and write it on the line provided. If you use word parts, underline the part you use.

Hints

Context clues | *Context* means the parts of a sentence or of a paragraph that come just before and just after a word. One kind of context clue is a definition or restatement clue.

Word parts | Words are made up of smaller units, usually a root word and sometimes a prefix or suffix. Readers often recognize parts of words because they are similar to other words the reader knows.

---

1. "One day the king spoke to his wife about Ntombinde. 'Where's her **modesty**?' he asked. 'How will we ever find someone to marry her? She's just too outspoken. She must get that from you.' "

   Definition _____

   Method _____

2. "For a *real* man, our daughter's courage and **outspokenness** will not be a threat."

   Definition _____

   Method _____

3. "The Snake Prince pulled in his tail and backed away. 'You're not big enough for a meal anyway,' the snake said **sullenly.**"

   Definition _____

   Method _____

4. " 'Then **controversy** set in,' continued the queen sadly. 'The younger children thought it unfair that their oldest brother was to inherit the throne.' "

   Definition _____

   Method _____

Moral Support

Myths and folktales can be entertaining and fun to read. They can also teach morals. *Morals* are lessons that readers learn from a story. You may be familiar with morals from stories you heard as a child. For example, "goodness is rewarded" could be one of the morals from the fairy tale *Cinderella*.

Directions: For each moral listed below, pick an incident from "The Snake and the Princess" that supports that moral.

Moral	Incident
1. Be careful what you wish for because you just might get it.	
2. Don't cut off your nose to spite your face.	
3. Greed can result in losing what you have.	
4. It is better to be yourself than to put on a false front.	
5. A secure person is not threatened by another's strong personality.	
6. Humans are basically good.	

Your Turn

Which moral do you think is the strongest in the story? Choose one of the morals from the above table or create your own. Then explain how it best represents the story.

READING FICTION SELF-CHECK

This self-check will help you keep track of your reading progress. The first three lines below each item list strategies that skilled readers often use. Mark how often you use each of these strategies.

1=almost always   2=often   3=sometimes   4=hardly ever

The blank lines are a place where you can add other strategies or feelings you have about reading.

Before I start to read a story, I think about

_____ why I'm reading this selection.

_____ what I expect based on the title.

_____ what I want to learn.

_____ _____

As I read a story, I

_____ try to find a character I can identify with.

_____ think about the relationships among the characters.

_____ think about the narrator's role.

_____ _____

When I come to a word I don't know, I

_____ see if I can guess the meaning from the words around it.

_____ ask someone or look it up.

_____ sound it out.

_____ _____

When a whole sentence doesn't make sense, I

_____ read it again.

_____ read the paragraph before the sentence.

_____ sound out the hardest words.

_____ _____

After I read a story, I

_____ talk to someone else about the piece.

_____ form an opinion about the piece.

_____ think about the themes, or messages, of the piece.

_____ _____

Each time you complete this self-check, compare your answers to the answers you came up with the last time you completed the self-check. Then answer these questions.

What is the most important thing you learned from your work with reading skills and strategies?

_____

_____

_____

Describe a time when you used one of these skills or strategies in another class.

_____

_____

_____

What is the most important thing you've learned about reading fiction?

_____

_____

_____

How much better are you at reading now than when you first took this reading self-check?

_____

_____

_____

What tips would you give another student who was having trouble reading a work of fiction?

_____

_____

_____

Reading Poetry

At first glance, poetry might seem hard to understand. That is because poets use language in special ways. They choose words for sound as well as for meaning. And they use literary devices such as rhyme, free verse, rhythm, and figurative language. Sometimes poets play with words and ideas in order to discover new things about a topic. For example, they might compare raindrops to human tears or a brightly colored bird to a rainbow. Knowing how to read poetry can make understanding it easy.

How to read a poem:

1. Decide what the poem might be about based on the title.

2. Read the poem aloud several times. Listen carefully to the sounds of the words. Think about how the words and the sounds of the poem work together.

3. Try to imagine the objects, actions, or scenes the poet is describing. Form a picture in your mind, if possible.

4. Be aware of punctuation. The end of a line doesn't always mean the end of a sentence. If there's no period, read on to the next line without a pause. If a line ends in a comma, pause briefly before going on.

5. Look at the form, or shape, of the poem. Decide if the way the poem looks adds anything to its meaning.

6. Check to see if the poet uses capitalization, punctuation, or spelling in special ways. If so, what does it add to the meaning of the poem?

7. Based on the details in the poem, try to find the poet's purpose or message. Some poets write to share their ideas or feelings about life. Others simply write to entertain.

As you read through a poem, you might find the Think-Along method helpful to note your reactions to the poem. Each time you read through the poem, add more thoughts to your Think-Along.

SNOW TOWARD EVENING

by Melville Cane

As you read: See how one reader used the Think-Along method with this poem.

Think-Along

Snow Toward Evening
by Melville Cane

Suddenly the sky turned gray;

The day,

Which had been bitter and chill,

Grew soft and still.

Quietly   5

From some invisible blossoming tree

Millions of petals cool and white

Drifted and blew,

Lifted and flew,

Fell with the falling night.   10

Okay, I expect the poem to be about a snowfall that takes place toward evening.

"Suddenly" is an odd start. Seems to suggest that something came before.

Line 2 is very short. Maybe it's placing importance on the words. Maybe because the day is what came before.

I like the contrasting image of the day in lines 3 and 4—bitter and chill (yuck) to soft and still (nice).

Line 5 is a one-word line, probably to emphasize how quietly this is happening.

An invisible blossoming tree? I wonder what this tree has to do with a snowfall.

The petals fall with the falling night. Now I understand the title "Snow Toward Evening." The petals are actually the snowflakes. The "tree" must be the sky then. Nice image.

I think Cane's message is that sometimes nature changes so quietly and almost invisibly that people don't always notice.

SKATER IN BLUE

by Jay Parini

As you read: Look for contrasts within this poem.

Skater in Blue
by Jay Parini

The lid broke, and suddenly the child

in all her innocence was underneath

the ice in zero water, growing wild

with numbness and with fear. The child fell

so gently through the ice that none could tell   5

at first that she was gone. They skated on

without the backward looks that might have saved

her when she slipped, feet first, beneath the glaze.

She saw the sun distorted by the haze

of river ice, a splay of light, a lost   10

imperfect kingdom. Fallen out of sight,

she found a blue and simple, solid night.

It never came to her that no one knew

how far from them she'd fallen or how blue

her world had grown so quickly, at such cost.   15

Understanding the Poem

Directions: In order to appreciate a poem, you must first understand it. These questions will help you determine the meaning of "Skater in Blue."

1. Which line reveals what "the lid" is?

   Ⓐ the ice in zero water, growing wild

   Ⓑ she found a blue and simple, solid night.

   Ⓒ She saw the sun distorted by the haze

   Ⓓ imperfect kingdom. Fallen out of sight,

2. Which line indicates that the child fell without making a splash?

   Ⓐ The lid broke, and suddenly the child

   Ⓑ so gently through the ice that none could tell

   Ⓒ she found a blue and simple, solid night.

   Ⓓ She saw the sun distorted by the haze

3. According to the poem, how could the girl's companions have saved her?

   Ⓐ They could have jumped in and saved her.

   Ⓑ They could have stayed close to her.

   Ⓒ They could have turned around.

   Ⓓ They could have run for help.

4. What word does the poet use to describe life on earth?

   Ⓐ distorted

   Ⓑ imperfect

   Ⓒ simple

   Ⓓ blue

5. What is the "blue and simple, solid night"?

   Ⓐ the dark sky

   Ⓑ the ice

   Ⓒ the water

   Ⓓ death

Your Turn

Question 5 has two possible correct answers. Explain your reasoning for the answer you chose.

Contrasts

Part of the appeal of "Skater in Blue" is the contrasts within the poem. A *contrast* is created when opposite words or ideas are placed side by side or near one another. For example, "wild" (line 3) contrasts with numbness (line 4). A person who is wild is overcome with emotion, while a person who is mentally numb experiences no emotion at all. Contrasts cause mixed reactions within the reader which can arouse the reader's emotions.

Directions: As you reread "Skater in Blue," underline any other contrasts within the poem. Then do the Your Turn that follows.

Skater in Blue

by Jay Parini

The lid broke, and suddenly the child
in all her innocence was underneath
the ice in zero water, growing <u>wild</u>
with <u>numbness</u> and with fear. The child fell
so gently through the ice that none could tell   5
at first that she was gone. They skated on
without the backward looks that might have saved
her when she slipped, feet first, beneath the glaze.
She saw the sun distorted by the haze
of river ice, a splay of light, a lost   10
imperfect kingdom. Fallen out of sight,
she found a blue and simple, solid night.
It never came to her that no one knew
how far from them she'd fallen or how blue
her world had grown so quickly, at such cost.   15

Your Turn

Based on the contrasts you've just located in "Skater in Blue," what do you think the poet's message might be? Explain your reasoning.

Determining Rhyme Scheme

Many poems have a predictable pattern of rhymes. For example, pairs of lines might rhyme or every third line might rhyme. Poems with a definite rhyme scheme are called *traditional poems*.

Free verse poems use rhyme more loosely. Lines may or may not rhyme. If rhymes are used, they don't follow a regular pattern.

Directions: Is "Skater in Blue" a free verse or a traditional poem? To find out, assign a letter to the rhyming word at the end of each line. For example, any word that rhymes with *child* would be given an *a*. The first four lines have been done for you. Note: You may have to use several letters of the alphabet to complete the rhyme scheme.

Skater in Blue
by Jay Parini

The lid broke, and suddenly the child	*a*
in all her innocence was underneath	*b*
the ice in zero water, growing wild	*a*
with numbness and with fear. The child fell	*c*
so gently through the ice that none could tell	5
at first that she was gone. They skated on	
without the backward looks that might have saved	
her when she slipped, feet first, beneath the glaze.	
She saw the sun distorted by the haze	
of river ice, a splay of light, a lost	10
imperfect kingdom. Fallen out of sight,	
she found a blue and simple, solid night.	
It never came to her that no one knew	
how far from them she'd fallen or how blue	
her world had grown so quickly, at such cost.	15

1. Based on the rhyme scheme, would you say "Skater in Blue" is a traditional poem or a free verse poem?

   Ⓐ traditional poem   Ⓑ free verse poem

2. *Internal rhyme* is rhyme that occurs within a line of poetry. Which line in "Skater in Blue" contains internal rhyme?

   Ⓐ line 2   Ⓑ line 6   Ⓒ line 7   Ⓓ line 11

3. What idea do you think the poet is trying to draw your attention to by including internal rhyme in this line?

   _____

SOUTHBOUND ON THE FREEWAY

by May Swenson

As you read: Figure out where the alien tourist is.

Southbound on the Freeway
by May Swenson

A tourist came in from Orbitville,
parked in the air, and said:

The creatures of this star
are made of metal and glass.

Through the transparent parts   5
you can see their guts.

Their feet are round and roll
on diagrams or long

measuring tapes, dark
with white lines.   10

They have four eyes.
The two in the back are red.

Sometimes you can see a five-eyed
one, with a red eye turning

on the top of his head.   15
He must be special—

the others respect him
and go slow

when he passes, winding
among them from behind.   20

They all hiss as they glide,
like inches, down the marked

tapes. Those soft shapes,
shadowy inside

the hard bodies—are they   25
their guts or their brains?

Understanding the Poem

In "Southbound on the Freeway," an alien hovers in the air, watching the activity on a highway below. The alien interprets what it sees according to its own understanding. For example, at the beginning of the poem the alien states that the creatures of this star are made of metal and glass. The alien is actually interpreting automobiles to be the creatures who inhabit the planet Earth.

Directions: Fill in the right-hand column of the table below with your understanding of the alien's interpretations. A list of suggested terms has been provided, but feel free to use your own as well. Note: Some terms may be used more than once.

Possible Terms

headlights and taillights	the planet Earth	tires	roads
human beings	windshields	alien	flashing light
parking lots	automobiles	police car	

Alien's Interpretation	Your Understanding
creatures (line 3)	automobiles
star (line 3)	the planet Earth
transparent parts (line 5)	
guts (line 6)	
feet (line 7)	
diagrams (line 8)	
long measuring tapes, dark with white lines (lines 8–10)	
four eyes (line 11)	
five-eyed one (lines 13–14)	
red eye (line 14)	
soft shapes (line 23)	
hard bodies (line 25)	

Point of View

The angle from which an author tells a story or poem is known as *point of view.* "Southbound on the Freeway" is written from the viewpoint of a "tourist from Orbitville." In other words, information in the poem is presented as it is seen and understood by an alien visiting Earth for the first time.

Directions: Imagine that you are the poet and that you've decided to write more about life on Earth from an alien's point of view. Write a brief "alien" description for the following familiar objects.

Familiar Object	Alien Description of the Object
a factory	
a stoplight	
a satellite dish	
a sports stadium	
a zoo	
a shopping mall	
a planetarium	
a radio tower	
a movie theater	
a roller coaster	

Poets often express personal opinions through their characters' viewpoints. What comment about modern society do you think May Swenson might be making through the alien's observations?

Ⓐ Aliens have no idea what life on Earth is like.

Ⓑ Automobiles are taking over the Earth.

Ⓒ Cars often overshadow the existence of humans.

Ⓓ Automobiles are more important to us than people.

Alien Inferences

An *inference* is a conclusion based on personal knowledge or on the evidence at hand. Often an inference is a combination of both.

For example, imagine that you and your friend are sitting in the classroom before class. Another student enters the room and says "hi" to your friend. Your friend blushes and can hardly reply. At this point, you are able to *infer* what's going on. You know that your friend has been acting distracted lately. You also just saw your friend blush when the classmate said "hi." By combining your knowledge and the evidence at hand, you can infer that your friend has a crush on the other student.

Directions: The alien in "Southbound on the Freeway" makes several inferences about life on Earth. Complete the chart below by identifying the alien's inferences and the clues on which they are based.

Topic	Inference the Alien Makes About the Topic	Clue(s) the Alien Uses
automobiles (stanza 2)		The automobiles are the only moving things the alien sees.
humans (stanza 3)	Humans are either the guts or the brains of the creatures.	
tires (stanza 4)		The tires move the creatures.
streets and parking lots (stanzas 4–5)	Streets and parking lots are what the creatures move on.	
headlights and taillights (stanza 6)		The headlights and taillights are on the outside of the creatures, and they light up.
police cars (stanzas 7–10) 1. red flashing light 2. status in society	1. 2.	1. 2.

THE STONE

by Wilfrid Wilson Gibson

As you read: Use the Think-Along method to help understand this lengthy narrative poem.

The Stone

by Wilfrid Wilson Gibson

"And will you cut a stone for him,
To set above his head?
And will you cut a stone for him—
A stone for him?" she said.

Three days before, a splintered rock   5
Had struck her lover dead—
Had struck him in the quarry dead,
Where, careless of the warning call,
He loitered, while the shot was fired—
A lovely stripling, brave and tall,   10
And sure of all his heart desired . . .
A flash, a shock,
A rumbling fall . . .
And, broken 'neath the broken rock,
A lifeless heap, with face of clay,   15
And still as any stone he lay,
With eyes that saw the end of all.

I went to break the news to her:
And I could hear my own heart beat

Think-Along

With the dread of what my lips might say;   20
But some poor fool had sped before;
And, flinging wide her father's door,
Had blurted out the news to her,
Had struck her lover dead for her,
Had struck the girl's heart dead in her,   25
Had struck life, lifeless, at a word,
And dropped it at her feet:
Then hurried on his witless way,
Scarce knowing she had heard.
And when I came, she stood alone—   30
A woman, turned to stone:
And, though no word at all she said,
I knew that all was known.

Because her heart was dead,
She did not sigh nor moan.   35
His mother wept:
She could not weep.
Her lover slept:
She could not sleep.
Three days, three nights,   40
She did not stir:
Three days, three nights,
Were one to her,

Who never closed her eyes
From sunset to sunrise,   45
From dawn to evenfall—
Her tearless, staring eyes,
That, seeing naught, saw all.

The fourth night when I came from work,
I found her at my door.   50
"And will you cut a stone for him?"
She said: and spoke no more:
But followed me, as I went in,
And sank upon a chair;
And fixed her grey eyes on my face,   55
With still, unseeing stare.
And, as she waited patiently,
I could not bear to feel
Those still, grey eyes that followed me,

Those eyes that plucked the heart from me,   60
Those eyes that sucked the breath from me
And curdled the warm blood in me,
Those eyes that cut me to the bone,
And pierced my marrow like cold steel.

And so I rose, and sought a stone;   65
And cut it, smooth and square:
And, as I worked, she sat and watched,
Beside me, in her chair.
Night after night, by candlelight,
I cut her lover's name: 70
Night after night, so still and white,
And like a ghost she came;
And sat beside me, in her chair,
And watched with eyes aflame.
She eyed each stroke,   75
And hardly stirred:
She never spoke
A single word:

And not a sound or murmur broke
The quiet, save the mallet-stroke.   80

With still eyes ever on my hands,
With eyes that seemed to burn my hands,
My wincing, overwearied hands,
She watched, with bloodless lips apart,
And silent, indrawn breath: 85
And every stroke my chisel cut,
Death cut still deeper in her heart:
The two of us were chiselling,
Together, I and death.

And when at length the job was done,   90
And I had laid the mallet by,
As if, at last, her peace were won,
She breathed his name; and, with a sigh,
Passed slowly through the open door;
And never crossed my threshold more.   95

Next night I laboured late, alone,
To cut her name upon the stone.

Identifying Important Details

"The Stone" is a lengthy poem with many details. Summarizing will help you identify the more important details of the poem's storyline.

Directions: Fill in the blanks to complete the summary below. You may be able to answer from memory. If not, refer to the poem and to the notes you made in your Think-Along.

The poem begins with a woman asking the narrator to cut a _____ for her

_____. Three days before, he was _____ when he was struck

by falling _____ at the _____ where he worked. The narra-

tor intended to break the news to the girl, but some poor _____ reached her

first. After she heard the news, the girl seemed to turn to _____. For the next

three days and nights, the girl was not able to _____ or

_____. And her tearless, staring eyes, which seemed to see nothing, actually

saw _____.

On the _____ night, the narrator began working on the stone, with the girl

sitting beside him. During this time, the girl never _____. The only sound was

the stroke of the narrator's _____. As he chiselled the stone,

_____ chiselled the girl's _____. Soon after the narrator fin-

ished his work, the girl _____. The next night, the narrator worked to

_____ her _____ on the stone.

THE STONE

Analyzing Motifs

The word *stone* appears first in the title of the poem. Ideas related to stone appear throughout the poem. An image repeated throughout a selection is called a *motif*. Each motif can develop many different meanings.

Directions: The first column shows several passages that contain *stone* and related words. In the second column, explain how each **bold-faced** word is used. (An example is done for you.) Then answer the question in the Your Turn box.

	Passage	Meaning in This Passage
example	" 'And will you cut a **stone** for him, To set above his head? And will you cut a **stone** for him— A **stone** for him?' she said." (lines 1–4)	**stone**—*a headstone for her lover's grave*
1.	"And, broken 'neath the broken **rock,** A lifeless heap, with face of clay, And still as any **stone** he lay, With eyes that saw the end of all." (lines 14–17)	
2.	"And when I came, she stood alone— A woman, turned to **stone:**" (lines 30–31)	
3.	"And every stroke my chisel cut, Death **cut** still deeper in her heart: The two of us were **chiselling,** Together, I and death." (lines 86–89)	
4.	"Next night I laboured late, alone, To cut her name upon the **stone.**" (lines 96–97)	

Your Turn
What do you think the stone in the poem's title means?

READING POETRY SELF-CHECK

This self-check will help you keep track of your reading progress. The first three lines below each item list strategies that skilled readers often use. Mark how often you use each of these strategies.

1=almost always   2=often   3=sometimes   4=hardly ever

The blank lines are a place where you can add other strategies or feelings you have about reading poetry.

Before I start to read a poem, I think about

_____ why I'm reading this poem.

_____ what I expect based on the title.

_____ what I want to learn.

_____ _____

As I read poetry, I

_____ try to see how the poem's form, or shape, relates to its meaning.

_____ think about how the words and sounds work together to create meaning.

_____ try to imagine the objects, actions, or feelings the poet is describing.

_____ _____

When I come to a word in a poem I don't know, I

_____ check to see if it is explained in a footnote at the bottom of the page.

_____ see if I can guess what the word means, or I look it up.

_____ sound out the word and try to guess the meaning from any prefixes or suffixes, or from the root word.

_____ _____

When I don't understand an image or a description in a poem, I

_____ see if anything in the stanza helps me figure it out.

_____ refer back to the title for clues.

_____ reread the image or description and try to relate it to my own experience.

_____ _____

After I've read the poem once, I

_____ reread the poem until I find a meaning that makes sense to me.

_____ reflect on the poet's message.

_____ form an opinion on the worthiness of the poem.

_____ _____

What is the most important thing you've learned about reading poetry?

_____

_____

_____

What tips would you give another student who was having trouble reading poetry?

_____

_____

_____

Reading for Information

Readers take different approaches to informational pieces. You might

- read what you enjoy or what interests you, whether it's *The Guinness Book of World Records* or real-life adventures

- read what you need
  —to fulfill an assignment
  —to complete a task
  —to answer your question(s)

Your reason for reading will shape the questions you ask as you read. Here are one reader's questions about the passage below. What other questions might you ask?

Passage

All day long in Fayetteville, North Carolina, it had been as hot and sticky as syrup. The air molecules seemed to move so slowly that nothing could possibly happen.

It was April 25, 1989, and Carl Boney and Michael Etowski, both fourteen, were riding the bus home from school....Later, the two boys would talk about how they both had almost missed the bus that day....

"The driver, Richard Perry, said he felt hot and tired from a field trip he had just been on. I remember that," Carl says. "I took a seat at the back of the bus with the older guys."

Think-Along

But something is going to happen, or this article wouldn't have been written.

What difference did it make whether they caught the bus?

So this starts off like a normal bus ride. But the driver isn't feeling well.

SAVING A BUSLOAD OF CHILDREN

from *Kids with Courage*
by Barbara A. Lewis

Reason to read: The bus ride home began like any other. But it turned into a terrifying trip.
As you read: Write or draw your thoughts about what's happening in the Think-Along column. (The model on page 61 shows a comment next to every paragraph. You might want to comment only when you guess what's happening next or have a question. You should make at least four comments.)

Passage

All day long in Fayetteville, North Carolina, it had been as hot and sticky as syrup. The air molecules seemed to move so slowly that nothing could possibly happen.

It was April 25, 1989, and Carl Boney and Michael Etowski, both fourteen, were riding the bus home from school. Although they attended different schools, they took the same bus; in fact, they had met there and become friends. The other 34 kids on the bus with them ranged in age from kindergarten through eighth grade.

Later, the two boys would talk about how they both had almost missed the bus that day. Carl was scheduled to stay after in detention for talking too much in class at St. Anne's Catholic School. He had also been caught drawing when he should have been reading. But he decided not to stay that night. He'd make it up another time. Toting his books under one arm, he swung his feet up onto the bus.

Think-Along

"The driver, Richard Perry, said he felt hot and tired from a field trip he had just been on. I remember that," Carl says. "I took a seat at the back of the bus with the older guys."

At the same time, Mike was preparing to leave St. Patrick's Catholic School. As he opened his locker to gather his books, he and his friends shouted insults at one another. Locker doors banged shut, pounded by a dozen fists. The boys joked and threw wads of paper back and forth.

Soon summer would arrive in waves of heat and sweat. Mike told his friends that he would be a lifeguard for the Boy Scouts at Camp Durrant. Between that and working for his dad's construction business, his summer was mostly planned.

When Mike finally ran out the front door of St. Patrick's, the school bus was already crossing the parking lot. Mike shouted and waved his arm, chasing behind the bus, accidentally stumbling over his huge feet. At the edge of the lot, just before the bus turned onto the street, the driver saw Mike and stopped.

Mike teetered down the aisle as the bus took off. He plopped into a seat at the back next to his friend, Jennifer. Sensing the approach of a chocolate attack, he reached into his pack and pulled out a Snickers bar. Jennifer jabbed his ribs. "Hey, give that to me. I'm starving."

Mike waved the bar just out of her reach. "No way. This is my dinner."

Mike remembers, "I was going to split it with her, but when she tried to snatch it all, I had to tease her a little."

Jennifer leaned over Mike and grabbed his arm, biting in the air after the bar. Mike laughed and switched it to his other hand. Jennifer wrestled his arm down, and the heat-softened Snickers smooshed between their hands. Dividing up the spoils, they giggled and licked the chocolate from their fingers.

Meanwhile, Carl was talking to one of his friends. He told him that he was on his way to his mom's day care center, where he would use the computer to run off her assignments for the next week. Carl loved fooling around with the computer.

The bus turned onto Rayford Road into busy rush-hour traffic. "A few minutes later, without any warning, I felt the bus weave to the right," Carl says. "I looked up and saw a utility pole ahead."

Mike felt the bus lurch, too. It happened so fast that no one had time to wonder. He turned away from Jennifer as the bus bounced up on the curb, then felt a jerking crash as it sheared past the utility pole and careened on down the road.

"I saw blue sparks and heard all this popping sound," Mike says. "I was slammed around. Then I jumped on the seat so I wouldn't get shocked. Everyone was freaking out. I looked up front. It didn't look like anyone was sitting in the driver's seat."

"I saw the bus was headed towards trees," Carl relates. Suddenly a memory flashed through Carl's mind: his brother, Larry, teaching him to drive a few months before. "I jumped up and ran to the front of the bus. And then I saw the driver was leaning to one side of his seat."

Without taking time to think, Carl struggled over the driver's body and forced his own foot down, shoving Perry's leg to one side. He stretched out the whole length of his five feet, two inches and jammed his foot on the brake. At the same instant, he grabbed the wheel and barely steered the bus away from the trees looming ahead.

But because Perry's foot was pressed heavily against the gas pedal, as Carl let up on the brake, the bus lunged forward again. Carl wrestled the steering wheel and steered the bus toward the stoplight.

Mike reached the front of the bus at this moment. He helped Carl to steer as Carl pressed on the brake a second time. Mike flipped the ignition off, and the bus slammed to a halt.

Children screamed, cried, and banged into each other. Mike shouted at the older kids to help the little ones off the back of the bus to a grassy yard at the side of the road. Carl helped the children down. Some of the children sobbed; some laughed hysterically and then cried.

Mike continues, "I turned around and looked at the driver. I shook him, and I saw he had a lump on his head. I thought he had probably passed out and then hit his head."

"There was a large man looking in the bus window. I shouted at him to help me get Mr. Perry off the bus. Together we dragged him outside and stretched him out on the grass."

Calling on his Boy Scout training, Mike treated the driver

for shock. "I raised his feet and loosened his shirt. He was hot, then cold and clammy. He wasn't breathing, but I felt a slight pulse. So I opened his airway and kept it open until the medics from Fort Bragg came.

"There were two nurses, a man and a woman. They put a neck brace on him. I don't know why they did that. I kept saying, 'Give him CPR,' while I kept him breathing. He was periodically coughing. They checked his heart rate and blood pressure.

"About then, the para-medics arrived, and they told me to beat it. They put electrodes on him and rushed him to the hospital."

As Mike stumbled onto the grass, friends pounced on him and Carl, smothering them with thanks and bear hugs. Only then did Mike begin to realize what had happened. He looked around. None of the chil-dren had been injured.

It turned out that Richard Perry had suf-fered a stroke while dri-ving the bus. Sadly, he never recovered. He died later in the hospital.

The day after Carl and Mike saved the bus and the children, their story was in all the newspapers. Many called the two boys heroes. Their classmates stared at them and whispered. And although the parents of the children who were on that bus would cer-tainly agree that the boys are heroes, both Carl and Mike deny it. "We're just ordinary boys," Mike says. "What we did was natural," Carl adds. In their own minds, they just did what needed to be done.

Reading for Detail

How exciting is this statement: "Two teenagers prevented an accident when a school bus went out of control"? The excitement in this selection is in the details the author provides. These details let you imagine what it was like to be on board that bus.

Directions: Choose the detail that most accurately completes each statement below. If you're not sure of the answer, go back and skim the article.

1. The school bus driver had a stroke just after

    Ⓐ Carl sat down at the back of the bus.

    Ⓑ Mike and Jennifer shared a candy bar.

    Ⓒ he went on a field trip.

    Ⓓ the bus turned onto a busy street in rush-hour traffic.

2. No one knew anything was wrong with the driver until

    Ⓐ he slumped down in his seat.

    Ⓑ the bus started drifting to the right.

    Ⓒ Mike jumped up on his seat.

    Ⓓ children started screaming.

3. Carl had trouble driving the bus because

    Ⓐ the driver was still in the seat.

    Ⓑ the steering wheel was so large.

    Ⓒ he could barely reach the brake.

    Ⓓ he didn't know how to drive.

4. Mike had to help Carl stop the bus because

    Ⓐ the driver's foot was on the gas pedal.

    Ⓑ Carl had to steer the bus away from some trees.

    Ⓒ Carl was trying to avoid a stoplight.

    Ⓓ Carl was trying to brake.

5. After the bus stopped, the first thing Mike did was

    Ⓐ call for help.

    Ⓑ give the driver first aid.

    Ⓒ ask the older kids to help everyone off the bus.

    Ⓓ feel like a hero.

Visualizing

Reading is like making a movie in your mind. Skilled readers create mental pictures from the words they read. They use pictures to bring the action to life. This activity will help you visualize the action in "Saving a Busload of Children."

Directions: Suppose that this story is going to be filmed for a television show about heroic teenagers. Write directions for the actors and film crew based on the passages below. Your directions should describe what you want the finished scene to look or sound like on film.

Passage	Directions
"Mike shouted and waved his arm, chasing behind the bus, accidentally stumbling over his huge feet."	Tell the actor playing Mike what to do and what feelings to show. *"OK, you're afraid you'll miss the bus, so you're running after it yelling…"*
"Mike felt the bus lurch, too….He turned away from Jennifer as the bus bounced up on the curb, then felt a jerking crash as it sheared past the utility pole and careened on down the road."	You plan to show the bus from the outside. Tell the person driving the bus during this stunt what to do.
" 'I saw blue sparks and heard all this popping sound,' Mike says. 'I was slammed around. Then I jumped on the seat so I wouldn't get shocked. Everyone was freaking out….It didn't look like anyone was sitting in the driver's seat.' "	Tell the sound effects people what to add to the sound track.
"[Carl] stretched out the whole length of his five feet, two inches and jammed his foot on the brake. At the same instant, he grabbed the wheel and barely steered the bus away from the trees looming ahead….[Carl] steered the bus toward the stoplight."	Tell the actor playing Carl what to do and what feelings to show.
"Mike reached the front of the bus at this moment. He helped Carl to steer as Carl pressed on the brake a second time. Mike flipped the ignition off, and the bus slammed to a halt."	Describe how you want the actor playing Mike to move.

WHAT IS A GANG?

from *Drugs and Gangs*
by Margot Webb

Reason to read: Have you ever thought about joining a gang? This author has something she wants you to know.

As you read: Decide whether you agree with the author's opinion about gangs.

It is estimated that there are nearly 55,000 youth gang members in the United States alone. Gangs in the United States range from small ones of only four members to huge groups that stretch across the entire nation. Their memberships run into the thousands. Large gangs usually have headquarters in cities like New York, Chicago, or Los Angeles, but they have branches in small towns across the country. Many of these gangs have become wealthy and powerful by dealing drugs.

Many people believe that gangs exist only in the big cities. They are mistaken. Their headquarters may be in New York or Los Angeles, but it is their business to create smaller branches in many smaller cities.

- Atlanta, Georgia: John belonged to a gang. He was shot in the back and died at the hands of a rival gang.
- Chattanooga, Tennessee: José was arrested for killing a sixteen-year-old girl from another gang.

Los Angeles police officers question suspected gang members during a riot. (Corbis–Bettmann)

- Davenport, Iowa: Justin Voelkers, Anthony Hoeck, and Jason Means were convicted of shooting and killing seventeen-year-old Michelle Jensen. They belonged to the Vice Lords, a gang that has been around Davenport for 30 years. It has chapters all over the Midwest.

There is no particular pattern to where gangs are found. They are all over the U.S. Most gang members wear special clothes or accessories or throw signs (use hand signs to identify themselves to each other and the outside world). They often use graffiti to warn other gangs of their power and to mark off their territory or turf. Gang members often have gang handles, names given to them by the gang, such as J. Dog or Loco.

Gang members may seem as if they have it made. They usually have money in their pockets, a supportive and protective group of "brothers" and "sisters," and an exciting lifestyle. What you may not see, however, is that violence is a way of life for most gangs.

Many gangs are armed with weapons such as guns and knives. Guns especially are necessary for gangs involved in drug dealing. They are used to protect the gang, get revenge, and protect the business. In 1991 there were over 350 gang-related killings in Los Angeles alone. Most people involved in these killings are gang members, but more and more frequently innocent bystanders are the targets of the bullets.

Who Joins Gangs?

Gangs consist of all kinds of people, regardless of age or race. There are specifically African American, Asian, Latino, and white gangs. There are racially mixed gangs. There are also boys' gangs and girls' gangs.

People who join gangs are usually looking for something they don't get at home: love, attention, protection, friends, structure, money, or power. Gangs offer a sense of security and strength. They offer their members the ability to contribute something, a feeling of control over what's happening in their lives. Gang members build bonds with each other; they look out for each other.

Gangs also require the complete loyalty of their members. Once you join a gang, you must comply with whatever they ask. You are no longer an independent person. You are one of a group. You put your life on the line for every member of that group every day.

In the words of Hershey McFarland, a member of the Imperial Gangsters, "What matters is, 'Is you down?' When we go out and mob somebody, you got to be out there with us, throwing blows, pulling the trigger." He was quoted in the *New York Times* in May 1994.

Initiation Rites

Gang initiations are difficult. First, you have to prove your loyalty to the gang, and that you are not weak or cowardly, by committing a crime. If you work in a restaurant, you may be asked to spill hot coffee on a customer or to spit in his food to prove that you want to join the gang. Or you may be asked to commit a more serious crime such as robbing a store at knife- or gunpoint or physically hurting someone. In one case, gang members stopped a car filled with teens and told the new member that he had to gouge out an eye of one of the car's captives with a screwdriver. "It's either him or you," he was told. The boy blinded one of the teens.

These acts are proof of loyalty to the gang. They show that you are willing to do anything the gang asks you to do.

In yet another initiation ritual, gang members form two lines facing each other. The initiate runs through the line. The gang members can hurt him in any way they like. This is called "walking the line." If you live through it, you are in the gang.

Gang Life

Once in a gang, you may think your life has become exciting. You live on the edge of the law. You walk around the streets as if you own them. You may also peddle drugs to young kids, lining your pockets with their money and their futures. You may feel on top of the world. You should also know that your life is in constant danger.

Drive-by shootings began as acts of revenge on specific people, usually rival gang members. Today, anyone can be a target. Most gang members have bad aim. You, as a gang member or not, could be walking alone or with friends or family and suddenly find yourself in the midst of gunfire.

Other drive-by shootings occur when gang members go to enemy turf and shoot into houses at random. Children who live in such houses are taught to crawl under tables if they hear gunfire. Thousands of children are killed in their own homes by drive-by shootings.

Turf wars are another fact of gang life. Gangs take certain streets or territories as their own. They make it impossible for anyone to walk in "their" area without taking the chance of getting hurt. Each gang has its own turf. Wars take place about "owning" streets. If a member of one gang crosses the turf of the opposing gang, bullets fly. Members become soldiers fighting to the death. There is danger on every corner. In the end, all they have is their turf, a street that never really belonged to them in the first place.

Sometimes gang members get so excited in defending their territory, or taking revenge on those who have crossed it, that they end up shooting their own members. The police in one large city claim, "Gang members are terrible shots." The shooters are often too young to handle the powerful weapons to which they have access. They don't receive the proper training, nor do they usually have the strength to use the weapon properly. Thousands of innocent victims are claimed by these shooters every year.

Committing crimes other than selling drugs is a major occupation of many gangs. In one city, several young gang members decided to steal from a convenience store late one night. The owner saw five members come at him. He reached into his drawer, pulled out a gun, and started shooting. He shot two kids before he was killed. Upon hearing police sirens, the three remaining gang members ran out of the store and climbed a nearby fence, hoping to get away before police arrived. One kid had holes in his sneakers. He found himself stuck on the fence while bullets fired by his gang and the police whizzed around his head. He was struck by one and fell, dead. The bullet belonged to one of his own gang members. He was killed by someone who was supposed to love and protect him.

Supporting Conclusions

Directions: Decide whether the following statements are true or false. Then use information from the article or your own experience to prove your answer.

1. Gangs use violence to control their own members.

   True   False

   Evidence _____

   _____

2. The police think gang shooters are excellent shots.

   True   False

   Evidence _____

   _____

3. Young people join gangs because they believe gangs have something to offer.

   True   False

   Evidence _____

   _____

4. Each gang tries to stand out from other gangs.

   True   False

   Evidence _____

   _____

5. Gangs engage in activities that require violence.

   True   False

   Evidence _____

   _____

6. Gangs always deliver the benefits members expect.

   True   False

   Evidence _____

   _____

Contrasting Gangs and Clubs

Millions of Americans belong to clubs and organizations. Some of these groups have ceremonies for bringing in new members. Others require dues. Some have nicknames for members or club officers. Some, like Little League, even have uniforms.

Directions: The chart below identifies five ways gangs differ from other clubs and organizations. Complete the chart by filling in the second and third columns. You may also want to add another characteristic to the first column.

Characteristic	Gangs	Clubs/Organizations
How you get into the group		
Activities of the group		
Role of the members		
Goals of the group		
Benefits of belonging		
Other		

Your Turn

Write a definition of a gang. Make sure your definition explains the difference between a gang and a club.

Taking a Stand

Sometimes authors try to write from a neutral or unbiased point of view. They present evidence for all sides of a question. This author, however, has a point she wants to make about gangs.

Directions: The chart below lists several subjects on which the author gives her opinion. Complete the chart by writing the author's opinion in the second column. Then give your opinion in the third column.

Subject	Author's Opinion	Your Opinion
1. Why people join gangs		
2. How gang members prove their loyalty		
3. Gangs and their turf		
4. A gang member's life		
5. Benefits of being in a gang		

MERCY RACE TO NOME

Prereading: Words in Context

Directions: The passages below are from the article you are about to read. The **bold-faced** words might be unfamiliar to you. Read the sentences in which the words are used. Then look over the definitions. Finally, use your knowledge of these words to answer the questions below.

Word(s) in Context	Definition
1. "Leonhard Seppala…had dug and pickaxed in freezing rain, run off **claim jumpers** with a shotgun, and taught himself how to race sled dogs."	During the Alaska gold rush, miners staked claims to land where they hoped to find gold. *Claim jumpers* stole land that had already been claimed.
2. " 'It's **diphtheria,**' [Dr. Welch] told the family. Not many hours later, the girl died."	*Diphtheria* is a dangerous, infectious disease. Victims run a high fever and have trouble breathing because a membrane covers the throat.
3. Young Togo "was a nuisance, trotting alongside Seppala's teams, bullying other **mushers** and their dogs out of the way."	A *musher* is a person who travels on foot over snow with a dogsled. The command *mush!* is often used to tell the dogs to go faster.
4. "They credited Kasson and Balto with the feat of stopping an **epidemic.**"	During an *epidemic,* a disease spreads so rapidly that many people have it at the same time.

1. Why do you think Leonhard Seppala was chosen to make a dangerous trip?

_____

2. Why do you think health officials were concerned about an outbreak of diphtheria?

_____

3. Explain whether Togo would be a good dog to lead a team of huskies.

_____

4. Review the words defined above. Then make a prediction about what the title of the article might mean.

_____

MERCY RACE TO NOME

by Charles J. Shields

Reason to read: Could one man and his best dogs stop an epidemic?
As you read: Notice how Seppala responds to challenges.

Christmas, 1924: A girl in Little Creek, Alaska, has a sore throat. She is the daughter of Leonhard Seppala, a Norwegian who had come to the Yukon to find gold. As a young immigrant, he had dug and pickaxed in freezing rain, run off claim jumpers with a shotgun, and taught himself how to race sled dogs. Now he is the most famous musher in the territory. He has won the All-Alaska Sweepstakes race three years in a row.

"It's probably not too serious," said Dr. Curtis Welch, snapping his bag shut. "Just follow the instructions I've written down and she'll be fine."

But her recovery was slow. And then in late January, another girl in nearby Nome, just a few miles from Little Creek, complained of a sore throat. She developed a high fever and a deep, hollow cough. Dr. Welch was surprised by how quickly the illness weakened its little victim. He made careful notes and checked his medical books.

"It's diphtheria," he told the family. Not many hours later, the girl died. Reports of other cases began coming in to the Board of Health.

Quickly the town officials shut down the schools, the movie houses—any place where people would normally gather. Word spread that nine out of ten people who contracted the virus would die.

Fortunately, health officials in Nome had a supply of *serum*, a fluid containing antitoxins that could be injected into the blood. But when they examined the small bottles, they made a discovery: The medicine was too old. Meanwhile, the number of cases was rising. Most victims were children.

The nearest supply of fresh serum was in Anchorage, 1,049 miles away. From there, the railroad ran west to Nenana, still 650 miles from Nome. The roads were buried by snow, but an airplane could pick up the supply at Nenana and fly it the rest of the way. However, daytime temperatures were 40 degrees below zero. Two airplanes were available, but both had open cockpits. In the sub-zero weather, a single-engine biplane probably couldn't make it.

The health commissioner asked Leonhard Seppala to come into Nome for a meeting. The official had an idea—a last-ditch one—but there seemed to be no alternative.

"The serum can be brought up to Nulato— can you go get it?"

Seppala would have to make a trip of 300 miles alone, pick up a small package, and then retrace his dangerous journey. The trail would have changed because of blowing snow; the stretch going around Norton Sound would be especially treacherous. Trails there went over ice that sometimes broke off and drifted into the Bering Sea. Stories told of mushers who had followed a familiar trail for miles, only to find themselves out on an enormous ice floe, surrounded by dark waves.

Seppala knew other mushers had already volunteered for the trip. "I'll go," he said, "if you think I've got the best team."

The commissioner told him to get ready.

A few days later, Seppala was out in the kennels feeding his dogs at 6 a.m. The phone in the cabin rang. All the dogs started barking. Seppala remembered years later, "They must have had their eyes on the cabin hopefully, for when I appeared, dressed for the trail, there broke loose in the kennel such excitement as I have never seen equaled, except perhaps at the time of the sweepstakes."

The Serum Drive, as it came to be known, had begun.

Seppala picked his 20 best huskies. He chose Togo to be lead dog. As a puppy, Togo had been difficult and mischievous. He was a nuisance, trotting alongside Seppala's teams, bullying other mushers and their dogs out of the way. Once, when left behind in the kennel, Togo tried jumping the seven-foot fence. He ended up hanging upside down by one gashed leg. After his leg mended, Seppala gave the husky a chance on his race team. Togo, who was just eight months old, went 75 miles the first day. Within a few years, he had been awarded more trophies than any other husky in the territory.

Seppala's plan was to arrive in Nulato with at least eight dogs. Exhausted dogs would be left at villages along the way to rest up for the return trip. Seppala also knew that a few might die

from accidents on the trail.

He left Nome the morning of January 27. Anxious residents showered him with words of encouragement as he pushed off with his dogs. Togo set the pace. That first day, they made 33 miles. Then the team warmed up and covered 50 or more miles every day. Seppala told teachers in the small villages they passed to close the schools—he'd be back that way with serum if any were needed. Unknown to him, the disease was spreading faster than anyone had expected. Almost 30 cases and several deaths had occurred already.

On the fourth day, Seppala started off for Shaktolik, a native village on the south side of Norton Sound. The wind blew hard at his back, and he crossed the frozen ice in good time. Then the dogs picked up the scent of another team and ran harder.

Seppala came upon a musher breaking up a fight among his dogs. As his team barreled past, Seppala thought he heard the man shout, "...serum—turn back!"

Seppala shouted at Togo to *"Gee!"*—Turn! but the other dogs resisted. It took a mile to swing back. The man was waiting for them. In his hands was a small package.

"Sickness is spreading fast," he said. "You were already gone when we started relaying the serum up here from Nulato." He put the package in Seppala's sled and handed him instructions for its care.

Seppala and the team had already come 43 miles that day. Night was coming on. Wearily, he turned the sled around toward Nome. "Mush!" Togo strained hard. The other dogs yapped in a chorus of bewilderment.

Now the wind was in their faces. They headed into a gale blowing at 30 degrees below zero. They struggled through the night, arriving at a cabin where they'd been less than 24 hours

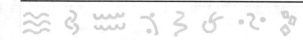

before. Without resting, the dogs had covered 90 miles. Seppala let them feast on salmon and seal blubber while he examined the package.

The serum was frozen.

"Make it as hot in here as you can," he told the cabin's owner. Gently, he put the package as near the fire as he dared.

After a few hours' sleep, he hitched the dogs back on the line. Time was critical. If he cut across Norton Sound instead of sticking to shore, he could save hours.

As the sled was being readied, an elderly man drew near shaking his head. "Ice not much good. Breaking off. Old trail no good. Go more closer shore." Seppala thanked him and waved good-bye.

Instead of listening to the warning, the musher chose to trust Togo's instincts. The husky led the team over the ice. When Seppala got to shore, he realized that the team had been running within a few feet of open water. His decision to cross the ice had saved two hours. But he and the dogs had barely escaped death in the freezing sound.

Hours later, Seppala met another sled sent out from Nome. His hands ached from gripping the sled. He found it difficult to speak. Togo and the other dogs had been running on bloody feet. The exhausted team had covered 340 miles in five days. Wearily, Seppala handed the serum over, and relay teams continued the race to deliver the antitoxin.

The serum changed hands 20 times between Nulato and Nome. The last man to take the serum into Nome was Gunnar Kasson. When the package reached him at 8 p.m., he took off. Traveling through the night, he covered nearly 60 miles. At 5:30 a.m. on February 2, his lead dog, Balto, brought the sled into town. Crowds rushed to help Kasson, who collapsed beside the sled, saying, "Fine dog, Balto, fine dog—you

brought us through."

Newspapers across North America picked up the story. They credited Kasson and Balto with the feat of stopping an epidemic. Meanwhile, Seppala, Togo, and the team returned to Little Creek after covering more than five times the distance of any other musher.

Kasson toured the country telling his story to paying audiences. New York City placed a statue of Balto in Central Park. A Hollywood movie studio made an adventure film about the Serum Drive starring Balto.

Seppala later observed, "I hope I shall never be the man to take away credit from any dog or driver who participated in that run. We all did our best. But when the country was roused to enthusiasm over the Serum Drive, I resented the stature [given] to Balto, for if any dog deserved special mention it was Togo."

The Serum Drive was Togo's last long run. Seppala took care of him into old age. One cold gray morning, Seppala wrote, Togo put a paw on his knee, "as if questioning why he was not going along with me. For the first time in 12 years I hit the trail without Togo." For the remainder of his life, Togo stayed at home in Little Creek. He sometimes posed for photographers with the many awards he'd won as a race dog.

Togo's valor has not been forgotten. Every year, a dog sled race between Nome and Anchorage follows the trail of the Serum Drive. It was first called the Iditarod, from the Eskimo word *Haiditarod*, meaning "far, distant place." In 1973, it was renamed the Iditarod Trail Seppala Memorial Race in tribute to a courageous musher and his team.[1]

---

1 Leonhard Seppala was the race's Honorary Musher from 1973 until his death in 1980. Since then, the Board of Directors chooses someone who has made a significant contribution to the sport of sled dog racing to be Honorary Musher #1.

MERCY RACE TO NOME

Accepting a Challenge

Directions: The chart below lists the problems and dangers Seppala faced on the Serum Drive. Complete the second column by describing how Seppala responded to the challenge. In the third column, draw a conclusion about what Seppala's response shows about his character.

Challenge	Seppala's Response	What This Response Shows About Seppala
example Health officials needed a volunteer to make a 600-mile round trip to pick up serum.	*Seppala accepted the challenge; he didn't claim he was the best man for the job, but agreed to go if the health commissioner thought his team was the best.*	*Seppala was a brave man who thought he could handle the trip. However, his many racing victories had not made him proud.*
1. Togo was unruly as a young dog.		
2. The trip was so dangerous that some of the dogs might not survive.		
3. Seppala was warned not to try crossing Norton Sound.		
4. Most of the credit for the Serum Drive went to Gunnar Kasson.		

Summing It Up

Directions: Suppose you are a radio broadcaster who has just learned that the Iditarod has been renamed. You want to give your listeners the most important facts about the race. You also want to include some interesting details. Complete the news announcement below by filling in the blanks. You may answer from memory or go back to the article.

This is _____ _____ with KBRR news on the hour.
(your name)

Since 1967, the annual 1,000-mile race from Anchorage to Nome has been known as the Iditarod. However, the Board of Directors has decided that the race will now be known as the Iditarod Trail _____ Memorial Race.

Leonhard Seppala was one of 20 mushers who delivered _____ to Nome during a 1925 diphtheria outbreak. Seppala risked his life to deliver the serum. He knew that the trail across Norton Sound was _____ up, but he chose to cross the ice to save time. He and his lead dog Togo covered _____ miles in five days. They then passed the serum on to a _____ team sent out from Nome.

However, the _____ gave all the credit to one team—Gunnar Kasson and his lead dog Balto. At the time, Seppala said, "I hope I shall never be the man to take away credit from any dog or driver who participated in that run. We _____ did our best. But…if any dog deserved special mention it was _____." Now race organizers are recognizing that Seppala and Togo covered more than _____ times the distance of any other team. The race's new name finally gives Seppala—and Togo—the credit they deserve.

DR. JACK HORNER

from *Succeeding with LD (Learning Differences)*
by Jill Lauren

Reason to read: Dr. John (Jack) Horner, the real-life model for the paleontologist in the movie *Jurassic Park,* had trouble with every subject in school. He even flunked out of college. Find out how he turned his learning difficulties into an unusual way of thinking.

As you read: Respond to the questions in the right-hand column. Feel free to write or draw other responses to what you read.

Passage

I remember as far back as second grade having difficulty in school. I was terrible at math, terrible at reading, and terrible with foreign languages—which I thought included English. I was terrible at everything. People didn't understand LD (Learning Differences) when I went to school. My teachers thought I was lazy. But I knew I wasn't. I thought they meant I just wasn't very smart.

I also remember being very interested in science. When I was eight years old, my father took me to a place near my home in Montana where he remembered a bunch of bones sticking out of the ground. While I was out there, I picked up a bone and gave it a number because I was already cataloging fossils. I thought it was a dinosaur bone and found out later that it was. I was so interested in dinosaurs and science that I thought about that stuff all the time, even in school.

In seventh and eighth grade, I remember wanting school to be over so I could get to the library. I looked at every science book in the town I lived in. Not only the ones in the library but also in the school, and in the libraries of the teachers and doctors. Every book I could find, everywhere. I never really read them, because I couldn't read. The pictures helped me learn a lot about science, though.

I also spent a lot of time wandering around the hills of Montana, looking for bones and fossils. If I could get some friends to go with me, that was good. But I didn't need to— I entertained myself pretty easily. I was still having a terrible time learning in school. But my mind was filled with questions about science, so I wasn't worrying about failing classes.

Think-Along

What's your first impression of Dr. Horner?

Dr. Horner couldn't read books on dinosaurs. How did he learn about this subject?

High school was the place where I could put my questions about science into action. Every year, we had science fairs. During my freshman year, I made a big rocket that went a long way. Everyone knew about my rocket, and I won the science fair. I didn't build it to impress anyone else, though. I built it because I thought it was pretty cool. I also won the science fair in my sophomore and junior years.

My senior project was about dinosaurs. I had been working on it since the tenth grade. I was curious about why dinosaurs in Montana were so different from the dinosaurs found in the same type of land formation in Alberta, Canada. That year, I won the science fair again. Two years ago, I finally published the answer to the question I was curious about. It took me all that time to find the answer.

Even though I was winning science fairs, I was still doing poorly in science classes. The teachers wanted us to memorize for tests. I can't understand what *memorization* even is. I don't think it's possible for me to learn to do it—it's just something I can't do.

My grades proved this. I only remember one B in my life. The rest were a few C's, mostly D's, and lots and lots and lots of F's. But I always believed in myself. This came from knowing that there were other things that I could do better than anyone else. My science fair successes and most of my successes in my career have come from an "I'm doing it my way" attitude. Finally, I graduated from high school with a D minus in English, and my teachers said they would have flunked me, but they didn't want me in there again.

I wanted to go to college because there were more books and more stuff to learn about science. I had lots of questions that I wanted to answer. Back then, some colleges accepted you even if you had bad grades, otherwise I couldn't have gone. Throughout college, I learned a lot but I kept flunking out. I still couldn't memorize. It was also hard for me to keep up with lectures. In chemistry, I remember my teacher writing on the board and talking about something else at the same time. I couldn't follow either. And I could never keep up with all the reading.

The college kicked me out for failing, but I kept going back. Then some teachers came to my rescue and said, "We don't know what's wrong with him, but he obviously has the

How long did it take Dr. Horner to answer his question about differences between dinosaurs in Montana and Canada? What does this show about him?

Explain why his "I'm doing it my way" attitude worked for Dr. Horner. How might this attitude work for you?

interest. We know he's bright, but he can't seem to get through these classes." I took every undergraduate and graduate course in science that I could find. It took me seven years to do this, but I never got a college degree because I had failed too many classes.

After I had taken every class I wanted to take, I wrote to English-speaking museums all over the world looking for any job related to paleontology. I was offered a job working in a museum in Princeton, New Jersey. At Princeton University, I became a paleontology preparator, which is the person responsible for cleaning and assembling dinosaur bones.

If I hadn't been offered this job, I still would have studied dinosaurs. I knew that I wanted to be someone who contributed something worthwhile to the study of paleontology. And I was hoping I could find something that would help unravel the mysteries of dinosaurs. Nothing would stop me from answering the questions I had.

While I was at the museum in Princeton, I learned about dyslexia and better understood what LD was. I was sort of relieved to understand there was a reason why school was always hard for me, but I had never let my LD stop me from doing what I loved in science.

Whenever I had a vacation, I went right back to the fields in Montana to explore and look for dinosaur fossils. On one of my vacations, my friend and I found something very exciting—nests that contained baby dinosaur bones. This let me know that baby dinosaurs stayed in their nests when they were young. This kind of behavior was unheard of in dinosaurs. It was big news, and lots of people all over the world wanted to know more about it. It took many years to dig up these nests, and we're still digging.

Eventually, I moved back to Montana so I could be near the fields. I became the curator at the Museum of the Rockies. I also teach at Montana State University in Bozeman. I never make my students memorize for tests. Instead, they have to explain what they know. Now I have an honorary doctorate from the University of Montana in Missoula, which was given to me by the same man who had kicked me out of college when I was younger.

Because I am dyslexic, I believe I offer a different

What do you think about Dr. Horner's idea of having students explain what they know instead of memorizing for tests?

approach to certain subjects. That comes with the way I think. I think differently, and that makes me ask questions differently. That's just the way some of us dyslexics are.

Information comes into my brain all jumbled up. I sort it out the best way I know how, and it may not always be sorted out right. I just line up the thoughts in the order in which I recognize them, until things make sense. When all the thoughts are lined up, I ask an original question. I don't sit around and think harder, I just think differently. Because I'm not able to remember everything, I tend to remember what's most important. Then I can get to the root of a problem, without overcomplicating things. People tell me I have an interesting perspective.

If I went back to sixth grade, I would probably get the same grades I got then. There's no way I could get higher grades, especially if the teachers still taught me the same way. But even with all my difficulties in school, I always did what I wanted to do. I wanted to be able to do real science. I wanted to be sure that I was asking good scientific questions and that I had the knowledge to try to answer them. I didn't know I could be paid to be a paleontologist, but I worked very hard to be one no matter what.

If you're interested in something, spend time doing it. It doesn't matter what the subject is. Don't worry about what other people say. With science, sometimes there's the stigma of being a nerd. Just don't pay any attention to that. If you're interested in science, do it. I feel good about what I do because it's exciting and fun. If you like what you do, then life is just a wonderful thing.

Why is asking questions so important to Dr. Horner?

Dr. Horner turned a learning problem into an unusual strength. Describe one of your strengths as a learner.

DR. JACK HORNER

Responding to Challenges

Dr. Jack Horner went from flunking out of college to being the real-life model for the paleontologist in *Jurassic Park*. The chart below lists some of the challenges he overcame.

Directions: Complete the chart by listing Dr. Horner's response to each challenge. You may want to reread parts of the article to find the answers.

	Difficulty/Problem	Dr. Horner's Response
1.	"My teachers thought I was lazy."	
2.	"I couldn't read [books from the library on dinosaurs]."	
3.	"I was still doing poorly in science classes."	
4.	"The college kicked me out for failing."	
5.	"I was sort of relieved to understand there was a reason why school was always hard for me...."	
6.	"Information comes into my brain all jumbled up."	
7.	"I didn't know I could be paid to be a paleontologist...."	

Interpreting Humor

Dr. Horner adds humor to his life story by using irony. *Verbal irony* occurs when a statement contradicts what is expected or what makes sense.

Directions: Read the ironic comments in the chart. Then, in the second column, write what you think Dr. Horner really means. An example is done for you.

Ironic Remark	What This Really Means
example "I was terrible at math, terrible at reading, and terrible with foreign languages—which I thought included English."	*Dr. Horner spoke English, but he found English class so hard that the subject might as well have been a foreign language.*
1. "I was so interested in dinosaurs and science that I thought about that stuff all the time, even in school."	
2. "...my teachers said they would have flunked me, but they didn't want me in there again."	
3. "Now I have an honorary doctorate from the University of Montana in Missoula, which was given to me by the same man who had kicked me out of college when I was younger."	
4. "People tell me I have an interesting perspective."	
5. "If I went back to the sixth grade, I would probably get the same grades I got then."	

A PLACE TO FIT IN

by Sandi Evans

Reason to read: Learn how Chinese American author Laurence Yep found a place to fit in.
As you read: Think about titles, or *subheads*, that might go in the numbered boxes.

The first stories Laurence Yep wrote were about space aliens. At first, he didn't realize that these fantasies reflected his own life. Later he recalled that he had often felt like an alien as he grew up: "I was the Chinese American raised in a black neighborhood, a child who had been too American to fit into Chinatown and too Chinese to fit in elsewhere."

1.

Yep was born in 1948 in San Francisco, right outside Chinatown. His parents owned a small grocery store, the La Conquista, in a racially mixed neighborhood. Black, white, Hispanic, and Asian all lived together. But the neighborhood began to change. As the whites, Hispanics, and Asians moved out, Yep's block got rougher. Sometimes gang members chased children out of the parks and broke into the liquor stores.

Yep first felt like an outsider here when some neighborhood children were playing war. The children were pretending to be World War II soldiers battling the enemy. They spotted Yep unloading groceries and made him their Japanese

Chinese seasonal workers wear traditional tunics and cloth shoes, but American-style pants and hats.

target. It didn't matter that he wasn't Japanese. To the young "soldiers," Japanese, Chinese, and Korean were all the same.

Yep didn't feel that he belonged at school either. Since he didn't speak Chinese, he often felt left out. He remembers that his classmates told dirty jokes in Chinese. Their teachers couldn't understand the jokes, but neither could Yep.

Yep's worst experience, however, came in the third grade. During a kick ball game, he threw the ball to a nun. She chose that moment to turn away, and the ball hit her in the head. Though she wasn't hurt, Yep's classmates wouldn't let him forget that he had hit a nun. He felt like an outcast.

2.

Eventually Yep found a sense of belonging at the public library. Reading had always been special to him. He loved the children's books and comics his parents had read to him as a child. The first big word he ever wanted to learn was in a Little Lulu comic. That word—*obnoxious*—was the first word he looked up in the dictionary.

When Yep went to the library, he wanted to find books about kids like himself. He wasn't interested in stories about children who lived in safe neighborhoods where families never locked their doors at night. He wanted to read about people who had the same problems he did. He discovered characters he could believe in one night during an asthma attack. His mother helped him through the attack by reading *The Pirates of Oz* aloud. Like all of the Oz books, this adventure occurred in an imaginary country. But the book seemed real to Yep because it was about children like him who had to adapt to new places and different customs.

Yep read first one Oz book, then another. And another. When his local library ran out of Oz books, he hunted more down in the Main Library. He moved from the Oz series to reading science fiction masters like Robert Heinlein and Andre Norton. Yep then expanded his world of books to bookstores.

Exploring bookstores, Yep discovered his love for history. He recalls, "I had discovered the secret pleasure of reading—of projecting myself in my imagination through time as well as space. As a result, facts and statistics became more than dry, dusty relics." They became fascinating pieces of a story—and he could become part of the stories he imagined.

3.

Yep began writing his own stories because of a challenge from his high school English teacher. Father Becker said that students could get an *A* in his course only if a national magazine accepted something they'd written. Yep's first story wasn't actually published until he was in college, but he got his *A*.

When Yep went to college, he had a hard time deciding whether to study chemistry or literature. He finally chose to major in journalism at Marquette University in Milwaukee. Then he realized he could combine his love for science and literature by writing science fiction. He sold his first science fiction story, "The Selchey Kids," when he was 18. He was paid a penny a word for it, which doesn't sound like much money. But, as Yep observed, it was the same amount Charles Dickens, a great writer of the 1800s, received for his work.

Yep wrote more short stories. When he sent them into the magazines, however, he got more rejection slips than acceptance notices. About three years after he sold his first story, his old college friend Joanne suggested that he write for children. Yep followed her advice and wrote his first science fiction novel. *Sweetwater* was a success. And so was his relationship with Joanne. Eventually they were married.

4.

Yep now tries to write four to six hours a day. He might spend another two hours taking notes and reading. He knows he must be disciplined and keep to a regular schedule to work successfully. "Writing a novel is a long process—like a long-distance runner running a marathon. I know that I cannot reach the finish line that day. Instead, I have to be patient, trying to complete a shorter stretch of writing—a chapter, for instance." Yep says that "I can only have faith that I will reach the end; and that belief keeps me plugging away for months to years to finish a draft of a novel—and a novel usually takes several drafts."

Yep is able to keep to this schedule because of the routine chores he had to do at his family's small grocery store. The long hours of stocking the shelves and balancing accounts at night taught him to stick to a task.

A peddler sells chickens in San Francisco's Old Chinatown, which Yep recreated in Dragonwings.

Working at La Conquista also taught him how to write about people. "I realized at an early age that what made people most interesting were their imperfections...I know that a character can come to life in a sentence if I can give him or her a 'quirk'—whether it's the way they look or dress, some habitual gesture, or some favorite phrase—that makes them special."

Yep bases some of his characters on family members and people he knew in Chinatown. In his autobiography, *The Lost Garden*, Yep writes, "My father, the kitemaker, became Windrider in *Dragonwings*. He had come to America at the age of ten but he did not like to talk much about the tough time he had had adjusting to life here." Yep used what he knew about his father to make the fictional Windrider "come to life."

Dragonwings was Yep's second novel. In it he recreates the characters and the life of Chinatown in the early 1900s. He got the idea for the novel when he read a 1909 article about Fung Joe Guey, a Chinese American who flew an airplane he had built. "When I first read

about...Fung Joe Guey, I could see his airplane turning over the hilltop. So I put that scene down on paper. However, it took me four years to explain why he was on top of that hill—and why he had built the airplane in the first place."

Yep took years to finish the novel because he spent so much time researching Chinese American history. He decided that he could answer his questions about Fung Joe Guey only by recreating the community the aviator had lived in. And that raised a new question. The first Chinese immigrants were men who spent years away from their homes. "What were personal relationships like among men who would work for five to ten years or longer before they could visit their families back in China?" The information Yep needed to answer this question was "scattered through several libraries in several cities." But he kept digging until he knew what it was like to live in Chinatown during the early 1900s.

Dragonwings was named a Newbery Medal Honor Book in 1976. Other honors include the Children's Book Award and recognition from the Jane Addams Peace Association, Friends of Children and Literature, and the *New York Times*. Yep has also received awards for *Child of the Owl, Sea Glass*, and *Dragon Steel*.

Yep continues to write about dragons today. His novels often have characters who wonder how they fit in with their friends and communities. And he is still exploring what it means to be Chinese American. His latest work, *American Dragons*, is a collection of stories about growing up Asian American. He chose stories that will appeal to readers like himself—people who want to find a place to fit in.

Analyzing Subheads

Articles in textbooks and magazines are often broken into smaller units, or sections. A title called a *subhead* tells readers what to expect in each section.

Directions: This biography of Laurence Yep has four empty boxes where subheads could go. For the first three subheads, select the answer that you believe best summarizes the section that follows. Use the last blank to write your own subhead for the last section.

1. *Subhead #1*

    Ⓐ Space aliens among us

    Ⓑ Feeling like an outsider

    Ⓒ Working in the family store

    Ⓓ Yep as a child and young man

2. *Subhead #2*

    Ⓐ Discovering books

    Ⓑ Learning big words

    Ⓒ Earning a living

    Ⓓ The Oz books

3. *Subhead #3*

    Ⓐ Becoming a writer

    Ⓑ Getting through school

    Ⓒ Lots of rejection slips

    Ⓓ Getting married

4. *Subhead #4*

    _____

A PLACE TO FIT IN

Identifying Cause and Effect

Directions: "A Place to Fit In" describes several things that influenced Laurence Yep's writing career. Some of these influences, or *causes*, are listed in the first column below. Complete the chart by writing the results, or *effects*, of these influences.

Cause	Effect
1. Some children playing war made Yep the "enemy," even though he wasn't Japanese.	
2. Yep didn't speak Chinese.	
3. Yep's mother read one of the Oz books to him.	
4. A teacher challenged (his students) to get something published in a national magazine.	
5. A friend advised Yep to begin writing for children.	
6. Yep read an article about a Chinese American who built and flew an airplane in 1909.	
7. As he grew up, Laurence Yep often felt that he didn't fit in.	

Compare and Contrast

Laurence Yep wanted to read about characters like himself. That's one reason many people read biographies. You'll probably enjoy biographies more if you look for things that you and the person you're reading about have in common. You can also find out more about yourself by looking for ways that you and that person are different.

Directions: Compare and contrast your life with the life of Laurence Yep by completing the Venn diagram below. Give five or six facts about yourself and five or six facts about Yep. Then note the similarities in the area where the circles overlap.

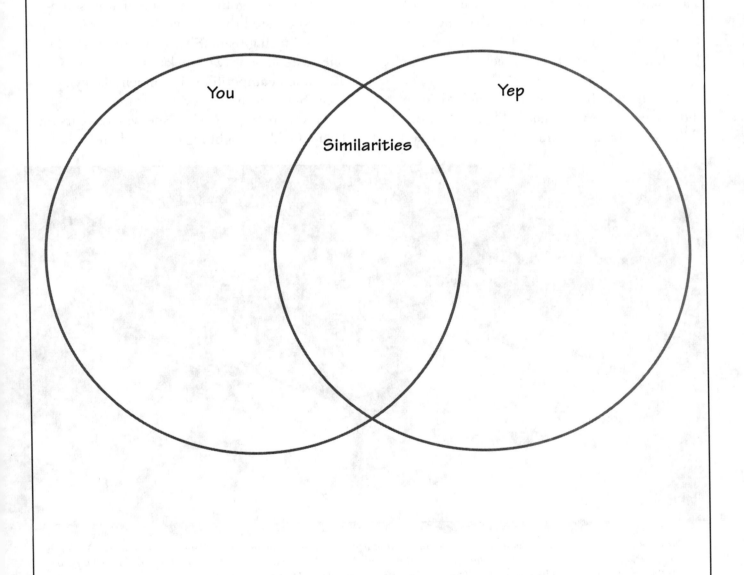

GOLDEN RULES

from *Champions*
by Bill Littlefield

Reason to read: Diana Golden is a world-champion skier. She is a superb rock climber. She climbs mountains, too, and enjoys five-day solo treks through some of the most unforgiving desert in the country. Also, she has only one leg, though she probably won't mention it if you don't.

As you read: Find out how Diana achieved her goal of being recognized as a world-class athlete.

Twenty-odd years beyond required gym class, Diana Golden still remembers what it felt like to be the last one picked for the basketball team, or the volleyball team, or any other team. "Come on," she used to say under her breath as the ranks of the unpicked grew thin, "pick me, come on."

According to her recollection, nobody ever did. That was part of what led her to embrace skiing as a child. You didn't have to be picked for it. You could do it by yourself. And it wasn't a required sport.

When she'd gotten pretty good at it, somebody suggested that Diana should try out for a kids' ski racing team. She made the team, but only lasted about two weeks. It was too serious. Too much competition. Too much like gym class. She returned to skiing for fun.

And then one day when she was 12 years old, Diana Golden's right leg collapsed under her.

Members of the 1988 U.S. Winter Olympics Team are honored at a White House ceremony. L-R: Debi Thomas (Bronze Medal figure skater), Diana Golden (skier), Bonnie Blair (Gold Medal speed skater), President Reagan, Brian Boitano (Gold Medal figure skater), Robert Helmick (President of the U.S. Olympic Committee), and Peter Oppegard (figure skater).

Weird, she thought. And then it happened again. When the doctors told her that the leg was cancerous and would have to be removed, she thought there had been some mistake. Cancer wasn't for 12-year-olds. "Did you ask my grandfather?" she said. Granddaddy was a doctor, and he'd certainly tell these younger doctors they were wrong.

"He knows," they told her. "He agrees with us. We're sorry."

Diana Golden remembers that, after her surgery, she was brave while her parents and the doctors remained in the hospital room with her. But when they'd left her alone with her roommate, she cried for two hours. She couldn't remember ever seeing anyone with only one leg. She was sure her life would be a hopeless muddle of crutches, braces, mechanical legs, and pity from all quarters. But eventually she ran out of tears, and her roommate said, "Hey, when you have a fake leg, maybe you'll be able to turn your foot around backwards." And Diana laughed.

Over the days that followed, it occurred to Diana to ask one of her doctors if she'd still be able to ski. "No reason why not," the doctor said. That helped, too. How could she feel too sorry for herself if she could still ski? And how could she feel sorry for herself when so many of the other children in the hospital with her would never enjoy that opportunity, or any other?

"I saw teenagers die," she remembered years later. "I saw a two-year-old die. *That* was the stuff that was hard to understand. Given those things, I never felt bitter, never wondered 'Why me?' I was *living*."

Within a few months after the removal of her leg, Diana Golden was back on the slopes. Of course she was still there on her own terms. She was a weekend hacker who liked skiing well enough to learn how to do it on one leg, but she was hardly inclined to train or work at it.

Through her first two years in high school, Diana Golden remained a weekend skier. She didn't train for competition, but given the circumstances, she couldn't help but develop some technique. As she has said since, "It didn't take me long to figure out there'd be no more snow-plowing."

One afternoon during the winter of her junior year, a fellow in a ski parka and goggles flagged Diana Golden down on the slopes. When she'd skied up alongside him, she recognized the man as David Livermore, the skiing coach at Lincoln-Sudbury High School in Massachusetts, where Diana was a student. "Listen," Livermore said to her, "why don't you work out with the ski team?"

"He recruited me," Golden said later. "He's a perceptive man. He realized that the training would make a difference to me. He understood when he saw me skiing that I'd reached a point where working out, training, and pushing myself wouldn't be drudgery anymore. It wouldn't be gym class. And he was right. It was fun."

Within a few months Diana Golden, who had never done a push-up or a sit-up, was embarrassing the two-legged skiers with her workouts. "All of a sudden," as Golden remembered during a newspaper interview with Melanie Stephens years later, "I began to discover that I could train my body. It was wonderful. It was discovering the things that my body could do for me, discovering what it felt like to be strong."

By the winter of her senior year, Diana Golden had left klutziness so far behind that it was hard to remember the bad old days. The rigorous training to strengthen her leg, her back, and her arms felt not only right, but indispensable. And the progress the training produced was nothing short of astonishing. Only a year after taking David Livermore up on his suggestion, Diana Golden was competing in the World Games for Disabled Athletes in Geilo, Norway.

Within the same year she won the downhill event in the World Handicapped Championships and became the brightest star on the United States Disabled Ski Team. She was skiing so well that, as *Boston Globe* sportswriter Tony Chamberlain put it, "She seemed *advantaged*." She had only one ski to worry about controlling, and she "moved back and forth down the hill with an unbroken motion as graceful as grass waving in a breeze."

That was, of course, an illusion. Skiing fast, like a lot of athletic feats, is harder than it looks. And skiing fast on one leg meant that Diana Golden had to cut from one edge of her ski to the other with more precision than most two-legged skiers could imagine. She had less margin for error because with one leg she had less opportunity to regain her balance when she lost it. Yet that sort of disadvantage never seemed to occur to Diana Golden. She was having too much fun to worry about it. She turned heads everywhere she skied, firing down the slopes like a wild bird, arms extended, snow flying everywhere. And the sense of fun was never eclipsed by the regimen of push-ups and sit-ups, or by the demands of competition. Once, at Vail, Colorado, when an out-of-control two-legged skier sent her sprawling and failed even to apologize, Golden bounced up, a look of mock horror spread across her face, and she shouted, "Hey, you! Look what you've done to my leg!"

[Eventually, Diana Golden began to race against two-legged skiers. At first, she had to race after all the other skiers had competed. By that time, the course was covered with ruts. Eventually the U.S. Ski Association] decreed that, after the top fifteen skiers had performed in a given race, places would be reserved for disabled skiers racing in the event. The new arrangement was not only a great leap toward fairness…it also provided a model for other sports that would encourage people to view all the competitors as athletes, rather than seeing some of them as courageous wonders or superhuman curiosities. Naturally the change was instantly nicknamed the Golden Rule.

…In 1986, Golden won the Beck Award as the best American racer in international competition. In 1988, *Ski Racing* magazine named her U.S. Female Alpine Skier of the Year. Also in 1988, the U.S. Olympic Committee named her Female Skier of the Year.

The titles Diana Golden had won were not preceded by words like "disadvantaged" or "disabled." She had simply earned recognition as the best there was at what she did—which is what she'd been after all along. " 'Courageous' is my pet peeve," she told Meg Lukens for an article in *Sports Illustrated*. "I think it belittles our ability. I never wanted to be thought of as having courage. I wanted to be recognized as a top-notch athlete, as the best in the world."

Sequencing

Diana Golden used to be considered a klutz. Then she learned to ski on one leg. Next, she set a new goal: becoming a world-class athlete.

Directions: The steps Diana took toward her goal are listed below. Number the steps in the order in which they happened. If necessary, skim parts of the article to determine the correct order.

_____ Diana's desire to ski helped her cope with the loss of her leg.

_____ She was named 1988 Female Skier of the Year by the U.S. Olympic Committee.

_____ She discovered she enjoyed feeling strong and became committed to training.

_____ She learned to ski on one leg.

_____ Her success influenced passage of the Golden Rule.

_____ She accepted the coach's invitation to work out with her high school ski team.

_____ Diana began competing against two-legged skiers.

_____ She began competing in races for disabled skiers.

_____ She won the 1986 Beck Award as the best American racer in international competition.

_____ She achieved her goal of being "recognized as a top-notch athlete, as the best in the world."

Your Turn

Based on these events, what goal(s) do you think Diana set for herself after she retired from competitive skiing?

Supporting Inferences

Directions: An *inference* is a conclusion drawn from facts. Below are several inferences about Diana Golden. Find statements or details from the article that support, or prove, each inference. A sample is done for you.

example **Inference:** As a child, Diana Golden was not very good at sports.

    Supporting evidence: *"Twenty-odd years beyond required gym class, Diana Golden still remembers what it felt like to be the last one picked for the basketball team, or the volley-ball team, or any other team."*

1. **Inference:** Diana's sense of humor helped her adapt to losing a leg.

    Supporting evidence:_____

_____

2. **Inference:** Diana refused to feel sorry for herself.

    Supporting evidence:_____

_____

3. **Inference:** Diana's skiing technique is better than that of most two-legged skiers.

    Supporting evidence:_____

_____

4. **Inference:** Diana does not think of herself as a disabled athlete.

    Supporting evidence:_____

_____

5. **Inference:** Diana has achieved her goal of being a "top-notch athlete."

    Supporting evidence:_____

_____

6. **Inference:** Diana changed her sport by showing that disabled athletes should be treated as true competitors.

    Supporting evidence:_____

_____

Summing It Up

Reporters can get the facts about any story by asking questions: Who? What? Where? When? Why? Reporters call these "the five W's." Good reporters don't stop there. They go on to ask "How?"

Directions: You can use these same questions to summarize the most important ideas in what you read. Use information from the story to answer the questions below.

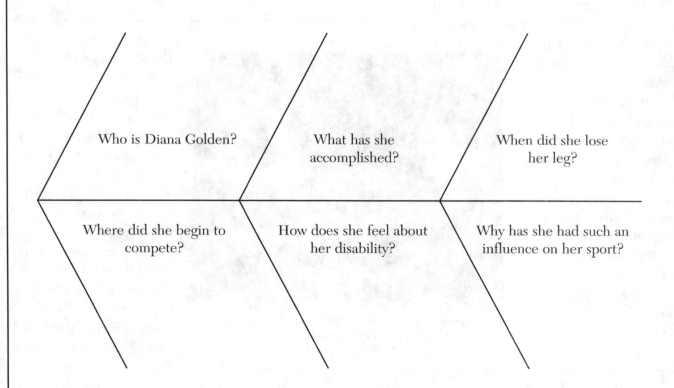

Who is Diana Golden?

What has she accomplished?

When did she lose her leg?

Where did she begin to compete?

How does she feel about her disability?

Why has she had such an influence on her sport?

MIND MACHINES

by Wim Coleman and Pat Perrin

Reason to read: Will computers ever learn to converse with people?
As you read: Look for ways that computers can and cannot "think" like humans.

1. Chess Match

The date was May 11, 1997. The sixth and last game in the chess match was over. Garry Kasparov, the world's Grand Master, resigned after only 19 moves. Three of the earlier games in the match had been draws, or ties. Kasparov had only won one game while his opponent had won two.

Now that it was over, Kasparov looked tired and unhappy. This was an especially painful match for him to lose. His opponent hadn't even been human. It was a massive computer. This was the first time a machine had ever defeated a grand master in a chess tournament.

The machine's proper name was RS/6000 SP. But it was more famous by its nickname—Deep Blue.

Deep Blue was born in the labs of Carnegie Mellon University in 1985. When Chiptest—Deep Blue's original name—was one year old, the computer competed in its first chess match. It's name was later changed to Deep Thought and finally to Deep Blue. Deep Blue wasn't much to look at, just a couple of big black boxes shaped like filing cabinets. Silent and expressionless, it could show neither joy nor sadness.

Nobody had tried to trick Kasparov into

Garry Kasparov watches Big Blue's chess moves.
Agence France Presse/Corbis-Bettmann

thinking he was playing a human being instead of a computer. But what if they had? Might he have believed he was playing some unknown human genius? Just how human *was* Deep Blue?

2.

These sorts of questions are asked by researchers in artificial intelligence, or AI. Alan Turing (1912–1954) was an early computer scientist interested in AI. He wondered if an electronic brain could do everything a human brain does. Aside from solving mathematical problems, could it also follow hunches or even feel happy or sad? Could it be self-aware, just like a person? Turing proposed a test to answer these questions.

Imagine you're in a room with a computer screen and keyboard. In a nearby room is a person sending you messages from his or her own screen and keyboard. In yet another room is a computer, also sending you messages. You are not told which messages are coming from the person or the computer. Your task is to figure out which is which.

You carry on typed conversations with the human and the computer. At the end of these

conversations, you decide which is the computer and which is the human. If you think the computer is human, Turing proposed, the computer has proven itself intelligent. It might as well be human. This kind of test is called the Turing Test.

3.

Turing himself worked out a chess-playing program on paper. So did German scientist Konrad Zuse in 1945 and Bell Laboratories researcher Claude Shannon in 1950. But these early chess-playing programs didn't worked very well.

In the meantime, AI scientists had been trying other things. By the 1960s, computers had gotten quite powerful. They couldn't play a good game of chess. But they could solve mathematical problems that no human could tackle.

Surely, AI researchers thought, such powerful machines could be taught to do things a toddler could do—recognize a human face, and speak and understand speech.

AI researchers were soon disappointed. Toddlers might not be able to do higher mathematics. But they could do lots of things that computers couldn't do. For example, one computer robot was programmed to pile up toy blocks, just like a small child. But the robot tried starting at the top of the pile. It dropped the blocks all over the floor! No toddler would make such a stupid mistake.

A robot named Shakey was somewhat more successful. Shakey was designed during the 1960s by a team at Stanford Institute in California. Shakey had a computer for a brain and a television camera for an eye.

He was sent rolling around a room filled with objects. Some of the objects were shaped like boxes, others like pyramids. Shakey knew how to tell boxes and pyramids apart. So when his operator told him to push a box, Shakey found a box

and pushed it. When he was told to push a pyramid, he found a pyramid and pushed it instead.

This kind of feat is called *pattern recognition*, and it made Shakey an important breakthrough in AI. Even so, it didn't seem all that impressive. It certainly couldn't compare to a baby recognizing its mother's face!

So, during the 1960s and 70s, research in AI seemed to have a long way to go. There was no question of a computer passing a Turing Test. After all, no computer could even begin to understand human language. AI researchers began to wonder if they would ever reach Turing's goal. Why was progress so slow?

4.

Some researchers suggested that AI was mistakenly taking a *top-down* approach. This meant that programmers tried to teach computers everything they needed to know. Shakey, for example, was programmed with information about boxes and pyramids. He could recognize these shapes but could not *learn* to recognize circles or ovals.

These researchers proposed a new approach to artificial intelligence. This approach grew out of advances in brain research during the early 1980s. The AI developers used this new information on the brain to create a device known as a *neural network*—or *neural net* for short. It was named after the *neurons*, or nerve cells, in the human brain. The brain consists of neurons connected to one another in incredibly complex ways. A single neuron processes information and shares it with other neurons. This process allows the human brain to learn. And without a programmer!

Neural networks were designed to imitate the brain. They are different from most computers. A typical home or school computer usually has a single processor. This processor solves problems *linearly*, or one piece of information at a time.

Neural networks, on the other hand, have many processors. These processors all work on a problem separately, then share their information, somewhat like neurons in the brain. This is called *parallel* processing.

You don't have to program a human brain. And you don't have to program a neural net, either. You give it a problem to solve and let it solve it. Just like a human being, it solves problems by hunches and by trial and error. It makes lots of mistakes along the way. But then, so do humans! This is called a *bottom-up* approach because the computer is starting from scratch.

This approach has had some remarkable successes. For example, Jordan Pollack of Brandeis University created a neural net that can play backgammon. Backgammon is somewhat like chess because it involves strategy. But it also involves chance because players begin each move with a roll of the dice. Single-processor computers have a problem with the element of chance. But Pollack's neural net, which taught *itself* the game, has gotten to be a very good player.

Neural nets can also do more useful work. They can match fingerprints to a database, grade potatoes, and monitor the production of steel. Others serve as robotic "brains" that drive cars. But even neural nets have not learned language, as Turing had hoped. No computer can fool a person into believing it is human. At least not for very long.

5.

Perhaps AI researchers shouldn't be disappointed. After all, a human brain contains about one trillion neurons. Each neuron can have thousands of connections with others. No computer is that complex!

Even Deep Blue is tiny compared with the human brain. The version which beat Kasparov had only 516 processors. These processors worked in parallel, but Deep Blue was not really a neural net. Its programmers used a top-down approach. They taught it rules and strategies piece by piece. It could not learn from its mistakes.

So why did Deep Blue beat Kasparov? It had power and speed. It was able to solve 50 billion chess positions every three minutes. This is called "brute force" computation. Deep Blue couldn't use intuition or instinct like a person. Instead, it treated chess as a huge math problem. It crunched numbers like no person can.

But *could* Deep Blue have passed a Turing Test against Kasparov? Perhaps it did. After the match, Kasparov seemed suspicious of the crew that handled Deep Blue. He doubted whether all the machine's decisions were mechanical.

One thing is certain, however. Deep Blue wouldn't have lasted a minute *talking* about chess with Kasparov. Not only did it not know how to talk—it never even thought about chess! It only crunched numbers. Even its inventors didn't credit it with real thought.

6.

Will a computer ever be built with the complexity of a human brain? Experts like computer scientist Hans Moravec and physicist Frank Tipler think so. If so, will these computers be able to think and feel? Will they be self-aware like us? Moravec and Tipler consider this certain too. Other scientists are doubtful. One thing is certain, however. Computers are destined to become faster and more powerful.

Perhaps some day a chess grand master will lose to a machine very different from Deep Blue. "Don't take it hard, old sport," the machine might say comfortingly. "You played a fine game. Better luck next time. And now—where could we go for a bite to eat?"

Alan Turing would be very pleased.

Analyzing Subheads

Articles in science textbooks and magazines are often broken into smaller units. Each unit, or section, is titled with a *subhead*. These subheads tell the reader the main idea they will find in this section of the article. This activity will help you recognize and write subheads.

Directions: In the article "Mind Machines," there are five empty boxes where subheads could go. For the first four empty subheads, select the answer that you believe best summarizes the section that follows. Come up with your own subhead for the last blank. An example for the first section of the article is done for you.

Example Subhead (based on the first section of "Mind Machines")

Ⓐ Garry Kasparov (Not a good answer because Kasparov is just one participant in the chess match.)

Ⓑ AI (This head is too broad for this section of the article.)

⬤ Chess Match (This is the best answer. The first part of the article describes the match between Kasparov and Deep Blue.)

Ⓓ Deep Blue (Not a good answer because Deep Blue is just one participant in the chess match.)

---

1. Subhead #2

   Ⓐ The Turing Test   Ⓒ Conversing with Computers
   Ⓑ Typing into Computers   Ⓓ AI

2. Subhead #3

   Ⓐ Slow Progress   Ⓒ Pattern Recognition
   Ⓑ Skakey's Success   Ⓓ Building Blocks

3. Subhead #4

   Ⓐ Backgammon and Chess Programs   Ⓒ Neural Nets
   Ⓑ Trial by Error   Ⓓ Bottom-Up Approach

4. Subhead #5

   Ⓐ Talking to Deep Blue   Ⓒ The Math of Chess
   Ⓑ Brute Force   Ⓓ Deep Blue

5. Subhead #6

   _____

Summarizing

Suppose you are asked to review the main points of "Mind Machines." How would you organize your thoughts? One quick way to review is to use a graphic organizer such as the one below.

Directions: As you saw in the last activity, the article has already been broken into smaller sections. By identifying the main ideas of each of these smaller sections, you can quickly review the entire article. Fill in the headings and at least two important details from each section of the article. The first section has been done for you as an example.

1. *Chess Match*

A. *The date was May 11, 1997.*

B. *Garry Kasparov, the Grand Master of chess, lost to a computer called Deep Blue.*

2. _____

A.

B.

3. _____

A.

B.

4. _____

A.

B.

"Mind Machines"

5. _____

A.

B.

6. _____

A.

B.

Completing a Timeline

A picture is worth a thousand words. This familiar saying is really true when it comes to charts and graphs. Charts like timelines convert numbers into pictures and make it much easier to see number relationships at a glance. In this activity you will chart some of the dates found in the article "Mind Machines."

Directions: The timeline below charts some of the important events in the development of artificial intelligence and computer chess programs. Use information from the article to place the events listed in the right-hand column into the blank lines in the timeline. Write the letter of the appropriate event on the blanks in the timeline. Note: Not all the events in the timeline appear in the article.

1945 _____

1946 Alan M. Turing develops a visionary design for the Automatic Computing Machine, which would be able to handle a variety of tasks—including chess-playing.

1950 _____

1954 _____

1960s _____

1973 Progress is made with brute-force calculations and better program design.

1980s _____

1985 _____

1988 Chiptest evolves into Deep Thought, the first computer to beat a Grand Master in a tournament.

1991 Deep Thought sweeps the American Chess Master championship.

1993 Deep Thought is redesigned and renamed Deep Blue.

1996 Deep Blue plays Kasparov and loses.

1997 _____

A	Deep Blue beats Kasparov at chess.
B	Alan Turing dies.
C	German scientist Konrad Zuse develops a computer program for making chess moves.
D	Chiptest—the original Deep Blue—is created in the labs of Carnegie Mellon University.
E	The first neural net is developed.
F	Researchers perfect Shakey, a pattern-recognition robot.
G	Bell Laboratories researcher Claude Shannon designs a chess-playing machine.

THE COW THAT CAN SWIM

Prereading: Setting a Purpose for Reading

Manatees, or sea-cows, are large, easy-going mammals. They've been around for millions of years. But they may not be around much longer. The article you are about to read contains the following information about manatees.

- Characteristics of manatees
- Problems humans create for manatees
- Efforts to save manatees from extinction

Directions: Make a list of questions you have about manatees. Then use your questions to set a purpose for reading.

My questions about manatees are

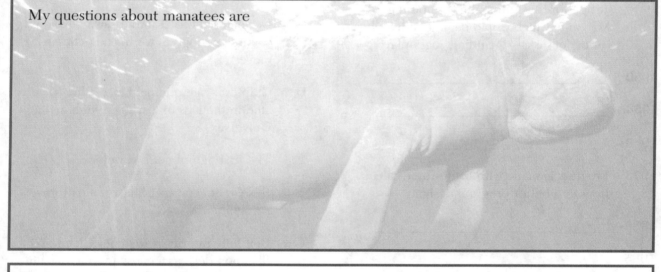

My reason for reading this article is

THE COW THAT CAN SWIM

by Nomi J. Waldman

Reason to read: Look for answers to the questions you have about manatees.
As you read: Underline or highlight the details that answer your questions.

Extinction is a scary thought. Any animal on the endangered species list is in danger of extinction; of disappearing forever. But as threatening as that sounds, it can also be a rallying cry, a challenge to do something to prevent extinction. Take the case of the cow that swims.

The Florida manatee, or sea cow, is a large, plant-eating mammal. Sometimes called "the gentle giant," the average adult manatee is about 10 feet long. Its average weight is around 1,200 pounds. Some manatees, though, can reach 13 feet in length and weigh as much as 3,000 pounds. Females are often bigger and heavier than males.

A manatee calf greets a diver.

Shaped somewhat like seals, manatees have paddle-shaped flippers in front and no hind limbs. The manatee uses its flippers and tail to steer, moving its tail up and down to propel itself through the water. A playful mammal, the manatee can do barrel rolls, stand on its head or tail, and glide upside down. Manatees even bodysurf.

Manatees seek places with warm water, shelter, and food. Summer months find them in the bays, slow-moving rivers, and coastal waters of Florida. Manatees spend about five hours each day feeding. They eat from 60 to 100 pounds of food a day—mostly sea grasses, freshwater plants, and even plants growing along the shore.

A manatee might spend anywhere from 2 to 12 hours a day resting. It can hang suspended near the water's surface or lie on the bottom for several hours at a time. Some manatees even lie on their backs underwater. Because it's a mammal, the manatee must surface every five minutes or so to breathe. (When they're resting, though, manatees can hold their breath longer.) When a manatee does come up to breathe, only its nose comes out of the water.

How did such a laidback, easygoing animal end up on the endangered species list? There may be fewer than 2,500 manatees in Florida waters now. Yet manatees have been around for millions of years. Why aren't there more of them? Part of the answer lies in the nature of the manatee itself. Manatees have a low birth rate. A female manatee gives birth to one calf every two to five years. But the main difficulties manatees face are human activities.

For thousands of years, humans hunted the manatee for its meat, bone, hide, and fat. Though now protected from hunters in this country, the manatee faces other dangers. These include any unusually cold winters, pollution, and poisonous red tides. Another problem is the continued development of Florida's shoreline. Such development can reduce the manatee's habitat.

The greatest cause of manatee deaths is collisions with boats and barges. A fast-moving boat with an inboard motor can run right over a manatee, killing it with its propellers. A barge moving through shallow waters can crush a manatee that has no room to escape. Even those manatees that survive bear scars and lasting injuries.

Human activity is the greatest threat to manatees. But it may also be humans that save the manatees from extinction. Efforts to do so began as far back as the 1700s. That's when the English established Florida as a manatee sanctuary—a place where these gentle creatures could be safe. Later, in 1893, the state of Florida passed a law to protect manatees. Other laws followed. Then, in 1978, came the Florida Manatee Sanctuary Act. This act made the entire state of Florida a "refuge and sanctuary for the manatees." The federal government also passed laws protecting the manatee and other marine animals.

In order to protect the manatee we must do research. The more we know about manatees, the better we can protect the species. The U.S. Fish and Wildlife Service and local agencies carry out research projects. Even corporations take part. Manatees like to hang around power plants in the winter. The warm-water outflow from the plants attracts them. That's how the Florida Power & Light Company got involved in manatee research.

Aerial surveillance is one way of learning where manatees go and what they do. Another is radio-tracking. This involves attaching transmitters to captured manatees before releasing them. A satellite in space then monitors the transmitters. Closer to Earth, there are telephone hot lines for people to report manatee sightings.

Manatees that survive boating accidents carry recognizable patterns of scars. Manatee researchers use the patterns to identify individual animals. They can then record each manatee's life history. For example, they might find out where a certain female spends each season. Perhaps they give her a name, like Rosie. They note whether Rosie is shy, playful, or outgoing. Then they follow the birth of Rosie's calf and observe it as it matures.

Education is another way of helping the manatee. As boaters are made aware of the habits of manatees, they can take measures to avoid hitting them. Many Florida waterways now have protection zones. Signs alert boaters to the presence of manatees and regulate speeds. "No Entry" indicates a manatee refuge. That means no boating, swimming, or diving. Other signs warn boaters to slow down because manatees are in the area.

Some organizations have set up manatee "adoption agencies." People are invited to contribute money for research and manatee protection. In return they get an adoption certificate and a picture of "their" manatee. Some of the money is used to rescue and treat injured manatees. Funds also go toward preparing educational materials and purchasing property for manatee habitats.

There are sites on the Internet that invite people all over the world to take part in these efforts. At one site, Net surfers can learn about manatee research. At another they might read up-to-date bulletins on manatee sightings.

So, with all these efforts, how is the manatee doing? At some refuges, the number of manatees has increased. This is especially true of less developed areas where there isn't a lot of boat traffic. That makes researchers hopeful. But it's too soon to predict if the manatee will be rescued from extinction. The only sure thing is that there's still a long way to go.

And we don't have forever.

Using Context Clues

Skilled readers can often find the meaning of unfamiliar words by using *context clues*. This means they study the way the words are used in the text. If that doesn't work, they can stop and look the words up in a dictionary. (In fact, skilled readers will often jot down new words and look them up later to learn even more about them.)

Directions: Use the context clues in the excerpts below to determine the meaning of the **bold-faced** words. Then choose the answer that best matches the meaning of the word. The first one has been done for you as a sample.

1. "Because it's a mammal, the manatee must **surface** every five minutes or so to breathe.... When a manatee does come up to breathe, only its nose comes out of the water."

   Clue: The last sentence describes what the manatee does.

   Ⓐ rise to the top   Ⓒ ride the waves

   Ⓑ swim strongly   Ⓓ exhale

2. "Another problem is the continued development of Florida's shoreline. Such development can reduce the manatee's **habitat.**"

   Clue: Manatees live along Florida's shoreline.

   Ⓐ life span   Ⓒ birth rate

   Ⓑ natural environment   Ⓓ playing time

3. "That's when the English established Florida as a manatee **sanctuary**—a place where these gentle creatures could be safe."

   Clue: The author gives a definition of the word.

   Ⓐ shelter   Ⓒ hunting zone

   Ⓑ study center   Ⓓ aquarium

4. "**Aerial surveillance** is one way of learning where manatees go and what they do. Another is radio-tracking. This involves attaching transmitters to captured manatees before releasing them. A satellite in space then monitors the transmitters. Closer to Earth, there are telephone hot lines for people to report manatee sightings."

   Clue: _____

   Ⓐ a bright explosion   Ⓒ a television camera

   Ⓑ observation from the air   Ⓓ the use of binoculars

THE COW THAT CAN SWIM

Making Inferences

Directions: As you read the following passages from "The Cow That Can Swim," look carefully at the author's choice of words and details. Use these clues to infer the answers to the questions that follow. (An *inference* is an "educated guess" or logical conclusion based on clues in a piece of writing.)

Passage 1

"The Florida manatee, or sea cow, is a large, plant-eating mammal. Sometimes called 'the gentle giant,' the average adult manatee is about 10 feet long. Its average weight is around 1,200 pounds. Some manatees, though, can reach 13 feet in length and weigh as much as 3,000 pounds. Females are often bigger and heavier than males."

1. How much do most manatees probably weigh?

   Ⓐ about 3,000 pounds   Ⓒ never more than 1,200 pounds

   Ⓑ more than 3,000 pounds   Ⓓ less than 3,000 pounds

2. Underline the words in Passage 1 on which you base your choice.

Passage 2

"Shaped somewhat like seals, manatees have paddle-shaped flippers in front and no hind limbs. The manatee uses its flippers and tail to steer, moving its tail up and down to propel itself through the water. A playful mammal, the manatee can do barrel rolls, stand on its head or tail, and glide upside down. Manatees even bodysurf."

3. What are manatees best suited for?

   Ⓐ living on land   Ⓒ living on land about half the time

   Ⓑ living in the water   Ⓓ living in a swamp

4. Underline the words in Passage 2 on which you base your choice.

Passage 3

"Some organizations have set up manatee 'adoption agencies.' People are invited to contribute money for research and manatee protection. In return they get an adoption certificate and a picture of 'their' manatee. Some of the money is used to rescue and treat injured manatees. Funds also go toward preparing educational materials and purchasing property for manatee habitats."

5. Why do some organizations encourage adoptions?

   Ⓐ so all manatees will have names   Ⓒ so tourists can take pictures of
                                            "their" manatees

   Ⓑ so people can feed the manatees   Ⓓ so people will continue to support
                                            "their" manatees

6. Underline the words in Passage 3 on which you base your choice.

Prereading: Mapping Knowledge

Authors who write about history usually write about the past. Newspaper reporters write about what's happening now. But authors who write about technology must cover the past, the present, and the future. They usually describe

- how things were done before the new technology
- what people can do with the technology now
- how this technology will change the future

Directions: Thinking about what you already know will help you appreciate how technology is changing firefighting. Use the boxes below to write what you know about fighting fires. One box has no label. You can give that box your own label or leave it blank.

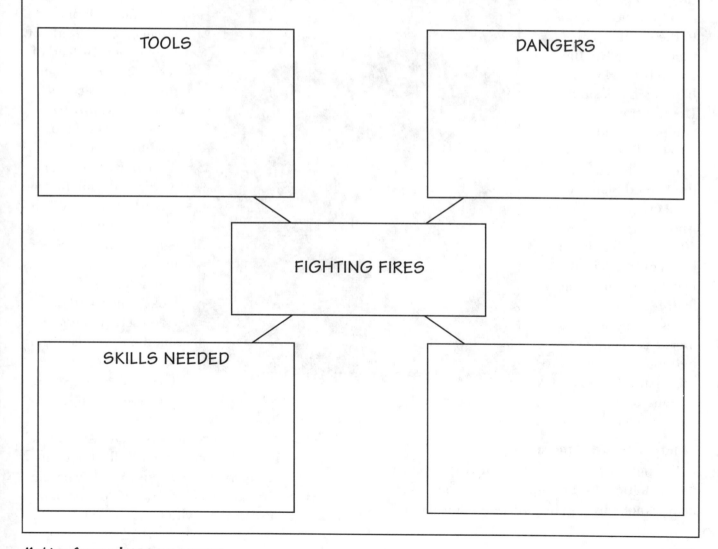

TOOLS

DANGERS

FIGHTING FIRES

SKILLS NEEDED

FIREFIGHTING GOES HIGH-TECH

from *Science World* (March 21, 1997)
by Emily Costello

Reason to read: Find out how new technology is making firefighting safer.
As you read: Identify solutions to problems faced by firefighters.

January 7, 1997—The emergency call rings at the Bethesda-Chevy Chase Rescue Squad. A house on Lindale Drive in Bethesda is on fire. Flames are leaping through the windows. A man may be trapped inside.

Jeff Hearle and his fellow firefighters grab their equipment, climb into the truck, and race to the scene. By the time they arrive, the house is filled with blinding black smoke. Hearle straps on his equipment and heads into the fire…

Fire kills someone in the United States about once every two hours. And last year, almost 100 firefighters were killed on the job. But new firefighting gear—high-tech clothing, ropes, hoses, and helmets—is making firefighting safer and more successful. Here's a look at some of the gadgets that might help firefighters save *your* life—and theirs.

Where There's Smoke . . .

Firefighter Jeff Hearle was lucky that January day. Traditionally, firefighters locate victims in heavy smoke by blindly sweeping their hands

along the floor. But that method is slow and dangerous. Instead, Hearle was outfitted with a new high-tech vision-enhancing helmet: the Cairns Infrared Imaging System (IRIS).

The IRIS consists of a flip-down display that fits over a firefighter's eyes, and a small black-and-white camera attached to one side of the helmet. Instead of recording *visible* light, this camera records low-energy *infrared* rays—light rays too long to be seen by the human eye. In other words, the camera records images of *heat*.

The infrared camera can "see" differences in temperature as small as half a degree. Fire looks white on the video screen; people stand out as relatively "cool" dark outlines. That makes it easy for firefighters to see—and save—people hidden by smoke.

"The IRIS gives firefighters their vision back," says George Bachelor, who works for the company that developed the system. While wearing the IRIS, firefighter Hearle was able to spot 40-year-old Guy Tayrien, who had passed out on his

kitchen floor. Hearle and his crew carried Tayrien to safety.

Firefighter Fashion

Even with the latest "heat-imaging" helmets, walking into a fire is dangerous. So firefighters suit up in pants and jackets made from Nomex fiber. This "super yarn" won't burst into flame, even in temperatures up to 371°C (700°F).

The material's resistance to heat, however, has created a new problem. Suited-up firefighters have a tough time telling when they're exposed to life-threatening heat. The result: More firefighters than ever are suffering from burn injuries.

So firefighters nationwide may soon be donning SmartCoats, coats rigged to warn firefighters when a fire is getting too hot, says John Cole of SunnyCor Inc., based in Washington, Connecticut. Here's how the "smart coats" work:

Each coat has silicone-capped sensors in the chest, upper arms, and upper back. Every five seconds, each sensor sends a signal to a *microprocessor* (computer chip) tucked away in the coat's lining. The microprocessor calculates how fast the temperature inside the coat is rising. When the temperature approaches 65°C (150°F)—slightly below the temperature that would cause blistering second-degree burns—the microprocessor sounds an alarm. That gives firefighters time to get out of the fire safely.

Let There Be...Rope?

Getting out of a smoke-filled building isn't easy. Firefighters usually use fire-resistant nylon or Kevlar rope to mark the path they've taken *into* a fire. That way they can retrace the path to safety. One problem: Drop the rope and you may never find it again...unless the rope glows.

That's why engineers at Flexlite in Edison, New Jersey, designed LiteLine—a kind of long, skinny, flexible flashlight. The "rope" is made of a series of tiny bulbs covered in tough, see-through plastic. The light can withstand immersion in water, and it won't melt, even in temperatures up to 232°C (450°F). And if flame does melt through the rope, the rope stays lit from the melting point back to the power source.

For firefighters, "it's like bread crumbs in the forest," says Paul Manley, Flexlite's president. Talk about bright ideas!

Targeted Splash

Soon, firefighters may not have to enter burning buildings at all, says Scott Kelly, a spokesperson for Charged Injection in Monmouth Junction, New Jersey. His company is designing a new nozzle that will enable firefighters to douse flames from as far as nine meters (30 feet).

The high-tech nozzle is called the Spraytron gun. It shoots water that's been exposed to a stream of negatively charged *electrons*, Kelly says. The electrons attach themselves to the water and give it a negative charge. The negatively charged water droplets repel one another and break up into a fine mist.

The charge also makes water from the Spraytron gun home in on fire—even under tables and in hard-to-reach places. Like an electric current, the charged water droplets seek out the ground, or any object—like fire—attached to it. So firefighters don't have to crawl into a burning room and aim the spray. Instead, they can slip the nozzle into the fire—and wait while it does the hard work!

The Spraytron gun might go to work soon aboard Navy ships crammed with valuable electronic equipment. And in a few years, the gun may be ready for use by firefighters around the United States, Kelly says.

Understanding Scientific Terms

Authors who write about science face a challenge: Most readers won't know all of the scientific terms they use. So writers often provide *context clues*, which allow readers to understand a word's meaning from the way it is used. Among the types of context clues are

- **definition.** The writer uses a word and provides its meaning.
- **comparison/contrast.** The word is contrasted to a word with the opposite meaning.
- **examples.** Details or examples show the word's meaning.

Directions: Complete the chart below by writing a definition of each **bold-faced** word in the second column. Then identify the type of context clue you used in the last column.

	Word in Context	Definition	Type of Context Clues
1.	"…Hearle was outfitted with a new high-tech vision-enhancing helmet: the Cairns Infrared Imaging System **(IRIS)."**	**IRIS** means	
2.	"…This camera records low-energy **infrared** rays—light rays too long to be seen by the human eye. In other words, the camera records images of heat. "	**infrared** means	
3.	"So firefighters suit up in pants and jackets made from **Nomex** fiber. This 'super yarn' won't burst into flame, even in temperatures up to 371°C (700°F)."	**Nomex** means	
4.	"Every five seconds, each sensor sends a signal to a **microprocessor** (computer chip) tucked away in the coat's lining."	**microprocessor** means	
5.	The Spraytron gun "shoots water that's been exposed to a stream of negatively charged **electrons,** Kelly says. The electrons attach themselves to the water and give it a negative charge. The negatively charged water droplets repel one another and break up into a fine mist."	**electrons** means particles that have	

Identifying Solutions

"Last year, almost 100 firefighters were killed on the job." Why is firefighting so dangerous? The answer is found in the way the author organizes this article. She states one danger or problem that firefighters face. She then explains an invention that helps firefighters deal with that danger.

Directions: The first column in the chart below identifies five problems that firefighters have. In the second column, explain the high-tech device that solves each problem.

Problem	Solution
1. Smoke makes it hard for firefighters to see.	
2. Firefighters risk getting burned.	
3. Heat-resistant suits make it difficult for firefighters to tell when they're near dangerous heat.	
4. Ropes used to mark firefighters' paths are hard to find if they're dropped.	
5. Getting close enough to the source of a fire to aim water at it can be risky.	

A GUN AT MY HEAD

from *Teenage Refugees from Bosnia-Herzegovina Speak Out*
by Valerie Tekavec

Reason to read: Find out how ethnic conflict changed this teenager's life.
As you read: Try to imagine how you would react to these experiences.

My name is Esmir. I live in Jacksonville, Florida. I came here from Mostar two months ago with my mother and my sister, Emza.

[A big explosion in Mostar on April 6, 1992, damaged all the buildings within 50 meters.] The Croats were responsible for the explosion. At that time, the military in Mostar was controlled by the Serbs; many of the soldiers were Serbs.

The first shooting in Mostar happened around April 10. It was nothing compared to those that came later. At first, I was so afraid that I couldn't sleep at night. Later, people got used to it; there was shooting all night and no one cared.

U.N. soldiers inspect bomb damage

Mostar is in Herzegovina, in a valley of the Neretva River. It is completely surrounded by mountains and hills. Like all cities in Bosnia, Mostar was very cosmopolitan. Muslims, Serbs, and Croats all lived together. There was also a small group of Jews. Before the war, Mostar's population was 150,000. It was the second-largest city in Bosnia-Herzegovina, after Sarajevo. Now only 40,000 people live there.

When the war started, the Croats controlled the area on the right, or eastern, bank of the Neretva, which was mostly Muslim. The Serbs occupied all the hills around the east side of the city. The Muslims on the western bank had very few arms, and it took the Serbs only fifteen days to conquer that part of the city. The west bank fell on June 15, 1992.

Our house was on the west side. On July 20, 1992, the Muslims and Croats led a big offensive and managed to liberate a tiny strip of land along the western bank. That was how we lived for one year.

On May 9, 1993, the second war, between the Muslims and the Croats, broke out and we were no longer allies. The eastern bank and parts of the western bank just along the Neretva were held by Muslims, but there were also 20,000 Muslims living in Croat-held parts. My house was right on the front line between these territories. I could look out on the front line from our living room. Eventually, the building I lived in was destroyed.

When the second war started, my father was wounded by an antiaircraft grenade that was fired into our apartment building. The big bullet went through the wall down to the floor, bounced back up through the door and into the hallway through a wooden chair my father was sitting on. It swept through the bottom part of both his thighs, and the chair shattered. All the little splinters of wood went into his legs. He got blood poisoning.

It was hard to get him to the hospital, because all the hospitals were on the Croat-held side. Six days later, he was transported to a provisional hospital on the western bank, but they had no medication. When the Bosnian Army

arrived, he was taken to a hospital on the eastern bank. He didn't get the surgery he needed until 15 days after being wounded. After spending two months in Mostar, my father was transported to a hospital in Zagreb, Croatia. Life for Muslims on the western bank was very difficult. There were about 20,000 of us on the west side of the river, and about 50,000 were in camps.

One day the Croats tried to seize our building. There had been shooting all day, and we had to go down to the shelter in the basement because all the windows faced the Croat side. You couldn't move your head for fear of being shot by snipers.

I am 17, but I look older. My mother was often afraid for me. The Croat soldiers came into the shelter with guns. When a soldier asked me my name, I said, "Esmir Celebic." Then he asked, "Are you Muslim?" "Yes," I answered. All the while, he was pointing a gun right at my head. My mother was clutching my arm. Then he asked me if I was in the Bosnian Army, and my mother said, "Oh, no! He's only sixteen years old!" My sister and I always tease her about how dramatic she is.

One day a boy from the Bosnian Army sneaked into the building and found us. He asked if we wanted to go to another part of town that was held by Muslims, a neighborhood called Cernica. This was all happening while my father was in the hospital; we had no idea how he was doing. To get across to Cernica, we had to cross a bridge.

Mostar had five bridges. During the first part of the war, the Serbs mined all the bridges in Mostar except the old stone bridge, built in 1566.

One day the old bridge was opened up to those who wanted to go to the east. That's when my mother, my sister, and I left. A few days later, it was closed again and we couldn't go back. We stayed with my father's sister, on the east side.

The streets were filled with soldiers. Every night they would look into the houses and search all the apartments. They were looking for arms and for men. Any men over 18 years were taken to the camps. We knew we had to leave.

The day I left Mostar, I went to my grandparents' house in a neighborhood called Brankovac to say goodbye. Brankovac was a famous Serbian poet from Mostar. He wrote during this century and was famous because he wanted Serbs and Muslims to be friends. The Turks had ruled Bosnia for 500 years. In the current war, the Serbs want to kill anyone who is a Muslim [for] revenge.

UN officials transported us out of Mostar. We went to Croatia. In Split, we applied to the International Rescue Committee for help, and now here I am in Jacksonville. My father is still in Zagreb. He's out of the hospital now and coming here soon.

My father is a professor of history. He taught at the University of Mostar. His field involved cultural societies of Mostar from 1900 to 1950. He was also the curator of the archives of Herzegovina. My mother used to do electrical drawings for buildings. She worked at that job for 22 years and then was fired because she was Muslim.

Before the war, I never felt any tensions between people. We had friends who were Croats and Serbs. People didn't care what you were. After World War II, when Yugoslavia was created, the only way to keep peace was to forget about nationalities.

I'm a senior in high school here…I got an A in calculus two weeks after we got here. At that time I was six weeks behind, so I think that's pretty good. I like my school here in the United States. I have made some new friends. I don't want to go back to Bosnia. I no longer have a home there. I don't have anything there. My whole family is here except for an aunt who is still in Sarajevo. None of my friends are there. Many of them will never go back. Mostar is dead now.

A Gun at My Head

Words in Context

Directions: Each of the **bold-faced** words below has several dictionary meanings. Choose the meaning that best fits Esmir's story. If you need more clues, find the word in the selection and reread the sentences around it.

1. "Like all cities in Bosnia, Mostar was very **cosmopolitan.** Muslims, Serbs, and Croats all lived together."

   Ⓐ widely spread over the earth

   Ⓑ universal; not limited to any one nationality

   Ⓒ courteous and refined

   Ⓓ worldly

2. "…The Muslims and Croats led a big offensive and managed to **liberate** a tiny strip of land along the western bank."

   Ⓐ free slaves

   Ⓑ release from combination with other chemicals

   Ⓒ steal

   Ⓓ free territory taken over by a foreign or hostile government

3. "You couldn't move your head for fear of being shot by **snipers.**"

   Ⓐ people who hunt snipes

   Ⓑ people who make nasty remarks about others

   Ⓒ sharpshooters who attack the enemy from a hiding place

   Ⓓ people who shoot targets one at a time

4. "During the first part of the war, the Serbs **mined** all the bridges in Mostar except the old stone bridge, built in 1566."

   Ⓐ dug for something valuable

   Ⓑ placed explosive mines

   Ⓒ took full advantage of a resource

   Ⓓ made a passage below the earth

5. "Any men over 18 years were taken to the **camps.**"

   Ⓐ areas used for camping

   Ⓑ people who have the same opinion about an issue

   Ⓒ temporary shelters for refugees

   Ⓓ places where military prisoners are held

Life Then and Now

Directions: The Bosnian conflict brought many changes to Esmir's life. The first column describes his life before the conflict. Complete the right-hand column by using details from the selection to describe his situation after the conflict. An example is done for you.

Before the Conflict	After the Conflict
example Muslims, Serbs, and Croats lived together in peace.	*Long-standing tensions erupted into a war of ethnic cleansing.*
1. Mostar had a population of 150,000.	
2. His father taught history.	
3. His mother did electrical drawings.	
4. Esmir's family was together.	
5. Esmir lived in a house near the front lines of the conflict between Muslims and Croats.	
6. Esmir thought of Mostar as his home.	

A GUN AT MY HEAD

Using a Map

Directions: Use the maps and their captions to answer the questions below.

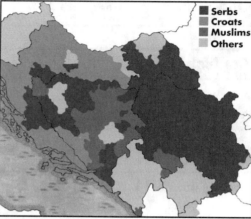

Most wars have two clear-cut opposing sides. The war in Bosnia-Herzegovina has three: the Bosnians, Croats, and Serbs. Sources of the tension include recent history, conflicting land claims, and religion.

- After World War II, a new nation called Yugoslavia was formed from six different nationalities: Bosnians, Croats, Serbs, Macedonians, Slovenes, and Montenegrins. Each of these nationalities has its own language, a distinct culture, and a fierce pride in its traditions.

- After Yugoslavia broke away from Soviet Russia in the early 1990s, each ethnicity wanted its own independent nation. Each group claims the land in Bosnia-Herzegovina as its homeland.

- Three major religions are devoutly practiced in Bosnia-Herzegovina: Eastern Orthodox, Roman Catholic, and Islam. Conflict among these religions has existed for centuries.

- Now some ethnic groups want to clear the area of other ethnic groups. This extreme and uncompromising effort to get rid of people who are different is called *ethnic cleansing*.

1. What do you think Esmir means by this statement? "After World War II, when Yugoslavia was created, the only way to keep peace was to forget about nationalities."

   _____

   _____

2. Esmir remembers that "Before the war, I never felt any tensions between people. We had friends who were Croats and Serbs. People didn't care what you were." Name at least two reasons that conflict broke out among Muslims, Croats, and Serbs.

   _____

   _____

   _____

   _____

You Wanted Our Country

from a speech to a missionary in 1792
by Red Jacket

Reason to read: Find out how the coming of the colonists affected American Indians.
As you read: Identify the most important changes the speaker mentions.

Brother! Listen to what we say. There was a time when our forefathers owned this great island [North America]. Their seats[1] extended from the rising to the setting of the sun. The Great Spirit had made it for the use of Indians. He had created the buffalo, the deer, and other animals for food. He made the bear and the deer, and their skins served us for clothing. He had scattered them over the country, and had taught us how to take them. He had caused the earth to produce corn for bread. All this he had done for his red children because he loved them.

If we had any disputes about hunting grounds, they were generally settled without the shedding of much blood. But an evil day came upon us. Your forefathers crossed the great waters and landed on this island. They told us they had fled from their own country for fear of wicked men, and had come here to enjoy their religion. They asked for a small seat. We took pity on them, granted their request and

The Seneca chief known as Red Jacket was famous for his speaking ability. His tribal name was Sa-Go-Ye-Wat-Ha, or He-keeps-them-awake.

they sat down amongst us. We gave them corn and meat. They gave us poison[2] in return. The white people had now found our country.

Tidings were carried back and more came amongst us. Yet we did not fear them. We took them to be friends. They called us brothers. We believed them and gave them a large seat. At length their numbers had greatly increased. They wanted more land. They wanted our country. Our eyes were opened, and our minds became uneasy. Wars took place. Indians were hired to fight against Indians, and many of our people were destroyed. They also brought strong liquor among us. It was strong and powerful and has slain thousands.

Brothers! Our seats were once large, and yours were very small. You have now become a great people, and we have scarcely a place left to spread our blankets.

---

[1] *seats:* lands or habitat
[2] "Poison" here means alcohol.

Understanding the Subject of a Speech

Directions: These questions ask you to identify the most important ideas in Red Jacket's speech. For each item, choose the answer that best expresses Red Jacket's message. If you're not sure of the answer, go back to the selection.

1. Red Jacket says that North America was

   Ⓐ waiting to be civilized by Europeans.

   Ⓑ once a useless wilderness.

   Ⓒ a gift from the Great Spirit to his people.

2. Before the Europeans came, American Indians

   Ⓐ often fought over hunting grounds.

   Ⓑ usually solved their problems without going to war.

   Ⓒ tried to claim as much land as possible for their nations.

3. When the whites came, Red Jacket's people

   Ⓐ shared land and food with the newcomers.

   Ⓑ ignored the colonists.

   Ⓒ tried to drive them away.

4. As more colonists came, Red Jacket learned that they wanted

   Ⓐ only a small amount of land.

   Ⓑ to tame the wilderness.

   Ⓒ more and more land.

5. The topic of Red Jacket's speech is best described as a

   Ⓐ prayer to the Great Spirit.

   Ⓑ summary of changes in the relationship between his people and the colonists.

   Ⓒ history of his people.

Interpreting a Metaphor

Red Jacket ends his speech with a *metaphor*, which compares two different things without using *like* or *as.* His metaphor gives an unusual meaning to a common word.

Directions: Analyze Red Jacket's use of the word *seats* by answering the questions below.

1. First use: "Our forefathers owned this great island. Their seats extended from the rising to the setting of the sun."

    Possible meaning: _____

    _____

    Clue(s): _____

    _____

2. Second use: "Your forefathers…asked for a small seat. We took pity on them, granted their request and they sat down amongst us."

    Possible meaning: _____

    _____

    Clue(s): _____

    _____

3. Third use: "…More [white people] came amongst us.…We gave them a large seat. At length their numbers had greatly increased. They wanted more land."

    Possible meaning: _____

    _____

    Clue(s): _____

    _____

4. Conclusion: "Brothers! Our seats were once large, and yours were very small. You have now become a great people, and we have scarcely a place left to spread our blankets."

    Another way to state Red Jacket's conclusion is _____

    _____

    _____

    _____

Analyzing Support for Main Ideas

Red Jacket made this speech to a missionary who believed he was bringing civilization to a savage wilderness. This missionary was convinced that European settlers were good for North America. How could Red Jacket persuade him that the arrival of the settlers was "an evil day"? Red Jacket used several examples to develop each of his important ideas.

Directions: Identify Red Jacket's examples by completing the chart below. You can use what you remember or reread parts of the selection. Finally, rate the effectiveness of Red Jacket's arguments on the scale at the bottom of the page.

Red Jacket's Point of View
The coming of the settlers was "an evil day" for the Senecas.

Main Ideas	Supporting Examples
The Great Spirit made North America for the use of his Indian children.	1. He created animals to provide food and clothing. 2. 3.
The colonists gradually took over more and more Indian land.	1. The Indians agreed to the colonists' request for a small amount of land. 2. 3.
The coming of the colonists was destructive to the Indians.	1. Instead of living peacefully together, settlers and Native Americans began fighting each other. 2. 3.

Your Turn
How convincing do you think Red Jacket's arguments are? Rate the effectiveness of his examples on the scale below.

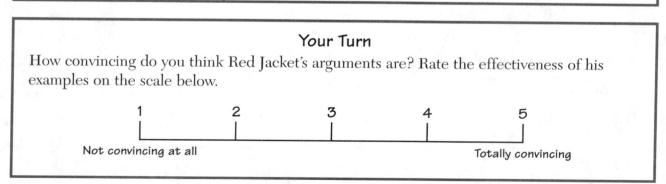

1   2   3   4   5

Not convincing at all   Totally convincing

A SOLDIER'S LAST LETTER

by Private Edwin R. Wakeman

Reason to read: Find out about what it was like to be in a Civil War battle.

As you read: Write or draw your reactions to this letter in the Think-Along column.

Letter

Grand Ecore Landing, LA
on the Red River
April the 14/64

Dear Mother and Father, Brothers and Sisters,

    I take my time to write a few lines to you. I am well and in good spirit and I hope these few lines will find you all the same.

    Our army made an advance up the river to pleasant hill about 40 miles. There we had a fight. The first day of the fight our army got whip[ped] and we had to retreat back about ten miles. The next day the fight was renewed and the firing took place about eight o'Clock in the morning. There was a heavy Cannonading all day and a Sharp firing of infantry. I was not in the first day's fight but the next day I had to face the enemy bullets with my regiment. I was under fire about four hours and laid on the field of battle all night. There was three wounded in my Co. and one killed.

    Albert Weathermax wounded in the head. Ranson Conklin wounded through the hip. Edwin West had one of his fingers shot off. Joseph Blanchard killed. That is all that was hurt in my Co.

    I feel thankful to God that he spared my life and I pray to him that he will lead me safe through the field of battle and that I may return safe home.

    I was glad to learn that you was agoing to work the Ham farm this summer and milk twenty cows. I could advise you to buy the farm and if you will, I will Come home and help you pay for it, if I live to get out of the army. By that time Robert will be big enough to do a good days work and he and my Self can work both of them farm like everything.

Good-by from your Affectionate,
Edwin R. Wakeman

Think-Along

What is your first impression of this soldier?

What was being in a Civil War battle like?

Comment on whether most soldiers would have had the same reaction to being under fire.

What else do you learn about this soldier?

Lieutenant "Harry T. Buford," shown in this 1876 engraving, was really Loreta Janeta Velazquez. As a child, Velazquez loved to read about soldiers. "Joan of Arc [who led the French army that freed Orléans] became my heroine, and I longed for an opportunity to become another such as she." When her husband, a Confederate officer, left to join his troops, Velazquez wanted to go too. But her husband refused to take her with him. So Velazquez disguised herself as a man and looked for ways to earn recognition as a soldier. Her first experience of battle was at Bull Run. Afterwards, she was eager to fight again. But she was sickened when her comrades shot retreating Union soldiers like fish in a barrel. So she became a spy. Velazquez volunteered for many other duties, until exposure during a harsh winter made her ill.

Your Turn

"Edwin R. Wakeman" was really Sarah Rosetta Wakeman, who disguised herself as a man and fought with the Union army. Private Wakeman survived this battle but died of illness in an Army hospital.

How does this information affect your reaction to this letter?

Reading for Historical Detail

Historians use two kinds of details to interpret Civil War letters. Some are clues found within a letter. Others are facts from sources outside the document. Both kinds of details are needed to understand this letter. For example, the date is incomplete. But the letter was written in Louisiana, which was given its name in 1699. So the battle could not have been before 1699. However, it could have taken place during the Civil War, which lasted from 1861 to 1865.

Directions: Choose the evidence that best proves each statement below.

1. The Battle of Pleasant Hill was not fought in 1964.

   Ⓐ The army retreated ten miles.
   Ⓑ The fight began at 8 A.M.
   Ⓒ Cannons were used during the battle.

2. Sarah Rosetta Wakeman had courage.

   Ⓐ She faced enemy fire for four hours.
   Ⓑ She thanks God for sparing her life.
   Ⓒ She hopes to survive the war.

3. Private Wakeman was one of many soldiers who used her wages to help her family.

   Ⓐ She sends best wishes to her family.
   Ⓑ She offers to help pay for the Ham farm.
   Ⓒ She encourages her parents to milk 20 cows.

4. The Battle of Pleasant Hill ended when darkness fell.

   Ⓐ Cannons fired all day.
   Ⓑ The battle lasted four hours.
   Ⓒ Private Wakeman had to spend the night on the battlefield.

5. Sarah Rosetta Wakeman did not plan a career in the army.

   Ⓐ Her brother is growing up.
   Ⓑ She hopes to live through the war.
   Ⓒ She looks forward to returning and working her family's farms.

A SOLDIER'S LAST LETTER

Making Inferences

Many questions about Sarah Rosetta Wakeman remain unanswered. For example, why did she decide to enlist in the 153 Regiment, New York State Volunteers? The only answers available are *inferences*—conclusions drawn from what is known about her life.

Directions: The statements below give facts about Private Wakeman and other female Civil War soldiers. Each statement is followed by two inferences. Choose the inference that fits the facts. Then write at least one detail that supports your answer, using the statements or the letter.

1. **Statement:** Sarah Rosetta Wakeman grew up in a large family that lived on an Illinois farm.

   Ⓐ Inference: Like most farmers at the time, she was probably poor and had little education.

   Ⓑ Inference: Her brothers taught her how to fight.

   Supporting detail(s): _____

2. **Statement:** Many soldiers sent their wages home to their families.

   Ⓐ Inference: Private Wakeman may have joined the Union army to help support her family.

   Ⓑ Inference: Private Wakeman planned to use her wages to go to college.

   Supporting detail(s): _____

3. **Statement:** Some women joined the Army to be with their husbands. But Sarah Rosetta Wakeman was not married.

   Ⓐ Inference: Private Wakeman probably enlisted for the same reason these women did.

   Ⓑ Inference: Women had different reasons for enlisting.

   Supporting detail(s): _____

4. **Statement:** Many male soldiers were so young that they didn't need to shave, and Army physicals were not very thorough.

   Ⓐ Inference: Women who tried to enlist were always caught.

   Ⓑ Inference: Sarah Rosetta Wakeman could have disguised herself as a male soldier.

   Supporting detail(s): _____

READING FOR INFORMATION SELF-CHECK

This self-check will help you keep track of your reading progress. The first three lines below each item list strategies that skilled readers often use. Mark how often you use each of these strategies.

1=almost always   2=often   3=sometimes   4=hardly ever

The blank lines are a place where you can add other strategies or feelings you have about reading.

When I come to a word I don't know, I

_____ see if I can guess the meaning from the words around it.

_____ ask someone or look it up.

_____ sound it out.

_____ _____

When a whole sentence doesn't make sense, I

_____ read it again.

_____ see if anything in the paragraph helps me figure it out.

_____ sound out the hardest words.

_____ _____

Before I start to read, I think about

_____ why I'm reading this selection.

_____ what I want to learn.

_____ what I might need to remember.

_____ _____

As I read for information, I

_____ first look the piece over to get an idea of what it's about.

_____ ask myself questions about what I'm reading.

_____ take notes on things I need to remember.

_____ _____

As I read biographies, I

_____ recall what I already know about this person or the time period.

_____ look for details that make this person come alive.

_____ try to find things I have in common with the subject of the biography.

_____ _____

When I read something about history, I

_____ expect that I might have to adapt to a writing style that's different from what I'm used to.

_____ look for clues about the time at which the piece was written.

_____ try to connect new information to what I already know.

_____ _____

When I read something about science or technology, I

_____ try to figure out how the writer organized the piece.

_____ make sure I know what each scientific or technical word means.

_____ try to connect new information to what I already know.

_____ _____

After I read, I think about

_____ the most important thing I learned.

_____ how what I learned relates to what I already know.

_____ whether I agree or disagree with the author.

_____ _____

Each time you complete this self-check, compare your answers to your answers the last time you completed it. Then answer these questions.

What is the most important thing you learned from your work with reading skills and strategies?

_____

_____

Describe a time when you used one of these skills or strategies in another class.

_____

_____

What tips would you give another student who was having trouble reading in social studies?

_____

_____

What tips would you give another student who was having trouble reading in science?

_____

_____

Text Acknowledgments